ce

THE FLIGHT PATTERN
TO ETERNITY

The Flight Pattern
to Eternity

A THEORY OF REALITY

by

Joseph Llewellyn White

PHILOSOPHICAL LIBRARY
New York

BD
331
.W5
1968

A Moment's Halt—a momentary taste
Of Being from the Well amid the Waste—
And Lo! the phantom Caravan has reacht
The NOTHING *it set out from—Oh, make haste!*

—Rubaiyat of Omar Khayyam (Fitzgerald trans.)

Contents

PART III
THE RELEASE FROM BLINDNESS

Introduction

WHAT INQUISITIVE mind has not asked: What lies beyond the universe, beyond the farthest galaxy? Is it a vacuum which extends into an endless night; or is it something that the mind cannot conceive, like an idea which has reached the point of absolute indifference—something which admits of neither wholeness nor disunity? Could it be a deity? Life has struggled from the beginning with a reality that constantly presses and closes in upon it. The fossils in the ancient rocks tell us that the history of life has been one of travail and that only the fittest have survived; but what is it that life in all its variety of numbers is trying to achieve? In short, what is the meaning of things?

The never-ending quest into the mystery of life and the riddle of the universe probably began with some long forgotten primitive man and is continuing today as the world seemingly grows smaller and man has just made his first adventure into outer space. In the longing to know the why, the how and the whereto of life and the universe, man has uncovered many of their mysteries and bound them into countless volumes. Man by his very nature must strive for a rational explanation of life in order to complete himself physically and ideally.

All systems of thinking are concerned with reality, for it is in reality that all things exist. Theories that are concerned with the nature of reality are rationalizations or assumptions of fact which must make a constant adjustment to the ever-changing conception of life and the universe; if they do not they fail to make sense. You are about to board a reality-vehicle which is bound for eternity in search of the

9

mysterious and the unknown with the aid of a practical pattern. Everything that you will experience is real; reality will never be, as Plato maintained, "a shadow cast upon the walls of a cave." Hegel insisted that "all that is, is rational," but I shall endeavor to prove that "all that is, is real."

Since the voyage will be long and, I hope, an enjoyable and exciting one, as your operator I must first tell you of what the vehicle consists. Reality will always consist of stages and phases, or phases and stages of lessening tension which are governed by a primordial and dialectical pattern as it releases the pent-up energy of life and the universe. The pattern will contain a triad of phases which will give direction to all the irrational wholes of the universe and also to all the rational wholes of life as the movements strive to complete themselves in either an ultimate or a hypothetical balance at the end of their theoretical tension line. The pattern will constitute the universal and the biological laws of consistency, and the stable and the unstable factors behind each whole of their movement will necessitate their continuance until the last line of tension is reached—which is eternity.

A practical pattern for all wholes of reality is difficult to formulate due to the problem of reconciling the irrational movement of the universe with the rational movement of life. Nevertheless, it will be our contention throughout the flight that both the decreasing wholes of the universe and the developing stages of life are seeking a completion by wholes of reality, and that each are equally real. Evidence will be gathered from the many fields of physical science to support the contention that there is a consistent and under-lying pattern which prevails throughout the movement of the universe, and later an effort will be made to prove that the movement of life is but the inversion of the universe and consists of phases and stages of lessening tension in all of its divisions, differentiations and specializations as that movement tries to complete itself.

The specific task of the voyage will be to reduce the complexity of life and the universe to their basic first principle; not to construct a model of life or to draw a blueprint of the universe. Every effort will be made to avoid over-simplification; however, the word metaphysics will mean basic first principle. Besides the task of determining the actual pattern used by life and the universe in creating all the wholes of their reality, a metaphysical framework will be constructed in order to determine the respective goals of each. It is rare that a system of thinking which purports to construct a metaphysical framework for both life and the universe has resorted to charts in order to outline their movements, but on the flight we shall have recourse to two charts. One will assist the voyager in visualizing the universal movement and the other will aid in the understanding of the three metaphysical movements of life and their relationship to the stages of the universe.

The pattern that is used on the flight to modulate the stages of reality must necessarily cross many fields of applied science, and for that reason it is doubtful that anyone is fully qualified for such an enormous task; but if the pattern being used is the one that is actually used by both life and the universe to create all the wholes of their reality, at least a broad outline of the movements should be discernible and for this reason we shall think of ourselves as astronauts viewing the earth from the moon—while being able to discern its general features we cannot resolve all its details. Despite the complexity of stages which hide the fundamental nature of reality, an endeavor will be made to explain the universe in terms of its reality, the relationship between the reality of life and the reality of the universe, and the function of feeling in the release of the life processes. While attempting no definition of life and the universe, it is hoped that, with the aid of a practical pattern which is valid for both life and the universe, a better understanding of the two movements will unfold. Students of philosophy will find the theory borrowing from many systems of thought with the ultimate view of uniting all systems into one general view of life and the universe. It is hoped that the scientist will find encouragement to continue his efforts to reduce the complexity of the physical world. For the growing num-

ber of laymen who are confounded by a world which seemingly grows more complex than simple, it is hoped that the
flight will afford a better over-all view of the direction of
both life and the universe and the significance it gives to
life as an ideal or spiritual movement.

Part I

THE FLIGHT FROM TENSION

CHAPTER I

Preface to Part One

TWO OPPOSITE reality movements which have a common pattern will be explored on our flight to eternity; one will belong to the universe and the other will belong to life. Part One, The Flight From Tension, will disclose the source of the universal stream; we shall follow its course until it flows into the sea of negation. Each stage and phase of the stream will comprise a decreasing whole of reality which is governed by a practical pattern. As we know the universe it is incomplete, and since stage after stage has to be torn down to rid it of tension, we call it irrational; but, actually, the goal of the universe is a return to a more normal condition, one that existed before its creation. In order to hypothesize the primal phase which existed prior to the creation of the universe, we shall have to go beyond the superficialities of the knowing world, with its complex systems of reduction, and project a world that is unreal and unknowable by means of a practical metaphysics. Such a state we shall imagine as a patternless stream of motion which has absorbed all the particles and waves of the universe into an ultimate negation but which, however, contains the indestructible factor of a purely creative phase.

CHAPTER II

Some Philosophies Which Have Influenced a Theory of Reality

HOW THE ABSOLUTELY rational became irrational or the absolutely irrational became rational in the first place affords wide room for speculation if we reject the "forbidden apple" theory from the start. Boehme, a medieval philosopher, believed that before the beginning of things there was an inexplicable factor present which caused a sundering to take place, and when it did the world was born. Long before the beginning of things, according to the philosopher Von Hartman, the world was at peace and will and idea were the same; but somehow, and unfortunately, they became separated and the Cosmos, the conscious world, arose from the separation with its increasing load of misery. He depicted cosmic history as from the Unconscious to Cosmos and back to the Unconscious. Von Hartman felt that God is now suffering in atonement for the separation, but that there is little he can do about it until the misery becomes so great the Cosmos will commit universal suicide. Then, he believed, will and idea again will be reunited and peace will return to the world.

Hegel reasoned that all that is, is rational, although not equally rational. Things are true, he said, only if they have an opposite, and he reconciled the difference in things as in the process of becoming; he used a triad whereby every movement has a thesis and an antithesis which, through the process of reasoning, resolves itself into a new synthesis; this rational process constitutes the Law of Inconsistency. The philosophy of Hegel is not evolutionary in the Darwinian meaning of the word whereby higher forms of life have developed out of lower and more primitive ones, but is rather a philosophy of the mind which he expanded to explain nature. Hegel saw the problem that besets the conception of reality in a greater perspective than any philosopher of his day, and by placing his Absolute Logos outside the reach of the grasping realist he was able to develop a pan-logism which would extend forever. But to do so he was compelled to guarantee a higher content by which differences could be reconciled. Thus his logos was a process and never an ultimate completion because an ultimate completion can never be attained by his Law of Inconsistency. He said that Absolute Being and Absolute Nothingness would be the same thing. The philosophy of Hegel contrasts sharply with the theory of reality advanced in this book.

The pessimist Schopenhauer believed the world to be absolutely irrational, the surface illusion of a blind and unreasoning will. Temporary escape from the misery of the world can be found in artistic contemplation, he said, but it is only a palliative; the only permanent escape from the misery of the world is by asceticism, or the complete denial of the will to live, and even this might not be of much benefit since man is so full of will. Schopenhauer borrowed his philosophy from the Orient as well as the Occident and highly regarded the teachings of Buddha because of its metaphysics. He declared: In thy nothing I hope to find the all.

The Church of the Middle Ages also believed the world to be an illusion, and members of the church were told to turn away from the illusion of the flesh and the devil and find reality in God. God, they said, can be found within by divine intuition and there is no need to look outside oneself for Him. Approaching the problem of reality from the opposite pole, the scientist of the past century believed that the reality of the world is fragmentary and incomplete; no matter how we try to conceive it, its randomness will always elude us. The difference between the two conceptions of reality may be expressed by means of a geometrical series: 1 plus $\frac{1}{2}$ plus $\frac{1}{4}$ plus $\frac{1}{8}$ plus $1/16$ etc. . . . . 2. To the churchman, the 1 and the fractions are unreal and only the

2 is real. To the scientist, the 1 and the fractions are real and the 2 is unreal. Since the older conception of matter as the basis of a physical reality was largely destroyed during the present century, a few scientists like Jeans and Eddington have attempted to combine a scientific realism with a form of mysticism to create an ideal concept of reality—in this case both the 1, the fractions and the 2 form a single concept of reality.

Those who believe reality consists of but one thing are called monists, and those who believe it consists of two or more things are called pluralists. The self-taught engineer Herbert Spencer declared himself a monist and expressed the belief that force or energy is the only indestructible thing in the universe. He did not, however, try to determine the direction of the mysterious force, nor could he state whether it is a material or spiritual manifestation. Spencer confined his pattern of integration-differentiation-determination to the universe and conceived force to be in a continuous state of redistribution; otherwise, it would destroy itself and there would be no basis for the Law of the Conservation of Energy upon which the physicist relies in the construction of matter.

Spencer's conception of reality was restricted but universal, while Hegel's was unrestricted and all-inclusive. On our flight we shall accept Spencer's supposition that everything in the final analysis is reducible to force or energy, but we shall reject his pattern; we shall accept Hegel's Absolute Logos only as hypothetical, and by offering a more practical pattern and by properly determining the respective goal of life and the universe we shall be able to construct a much clearer picture of both realities.

CHAPTER III

Facts or Speculations of Science Which Have Contributed to a Theory of Reality

SHOULD the cosmogonist wish to piece together the history of the universe, he has several possibilities open for consideration. To start with, he could theorize that there may have been only one universe and compare its beginning to a rocket that was launched into space by some unknown means. He could imagine that after the device reached the highest point of its projectory it exploded, causing a vast display of fireworks; then it began to disintegrate and is now burning itself into ashes and someday will disappear forever. Such a theory may be regarded as an ultimate universe, but the unknown means by which it came about forever clouds the theory in a mystery.

Instead of entertaining such a fantastic theory as to the origin, development and destruction of the universe, the cosmogonist might lean towards a theory advanced by Dr. Hoyle and others and regard the universe as a stabilized star system. Although Hoyle has altered his theory somewhat in recent years, he believed for a long time that the universe is able to perpetuate itself by spinning new stars, spiderwise, out of its own substance. There is evidence of the birth and death of stars in the universe. Some of the nebulae are apparently creating new stars out of the surrounding dust clouds, possibly by means of high energy interactions, while other stars seem to be dying, the flare-up of novae are thought to be the convulsions of dying suns. Dr. Hoyle's theory is noteworthy on our journey to eternity in that it recognizes the need for the reversal of the universal pattern of destruction in order to create new matter.

Perhaps the cosmogonist does not like either of the two above theories and regards the universe as an expanding system which keeps extending itself until finally it plays itself out, after which it begins to contract until its substance is condensed into a very small mass. Dr. Gamow has taken considerable pains to explain how some powerfully energetic substance could have formed the basis for all the elements in the universe within a matter of hours, and how it might have taken only a few hundred million years to create all the galaxies. By injecting the factor of primordial substance into the theory of the origin of the universe, Dr. Gamow has a scheme which is somewhat less mysterious than the other two; from it a timetable can be constructed for the completion of the entire universal system.

As man has probed into the vastness of space and the minuteness of the atom he has enlarged upon his conception of the physical world. The successful explosion of the atom bomb and the verification of the laws of relativity brought recognition to the theoretical physicist, and he is now in the forefront of the quest into the ultimate nature of matter. Little was known until recent decades concerning the inner nucleus of the atom, but it is now believed that it consists of particles which have high energy interactions. One such particle is the neutrino, which is so powerful that it can pass through a body ten times the size of the earth without having an effect upon it. The neutrino falls under the classification of scientific objects which can neither be seen nor felt; it is only recognizable by the tracks it leaves in a bubble chamber when by chance it collides with more recognizable particles which split into other plus and minus particles of the physical processes. All physical bodies, according to the Law of Parity, must have an antibody, and when it was discovered that the neutrino was no longer theoretical but an actuality many physicists believed that it might be the primordial substance of which all physical objects are composed —in short, the basic unit of the cosmos. However, it was fortunate for science, with its present incomplete conception of the universe, that the neutrino was found soon after its discovery to split into other plus and minus particles as the physical processes continued to maintain their general state of balances, for the Law of Parity was saved, at least for the time being.

While there is little known concerning the primal beginning of high energy particles, there is a considerable knowledge about the construction of the atom itself. The atom is the smallest unitary constituent of a chemical element, and is composed of a more or less complex aggregate of protons, neutrons, and electrons. The positive charge contained in the proton of the atom is the most important part of the atom and the number of protons determines the element. They vary from one for hydrogen to ninety-two for uranium. There is an underlying simplicity in the periodic table of elements which has led many physicists to believe there is a consistent pattern that pervades all nature. All of Einstein's work was aimed at expressing this. Yet, the more the physicist delves into the ultimate nature of matter the more mysterious matter seems to be. Since the outer limits of scientific research have probably already been reached, some believe that the next great scientific advance will be the discovery of the simple and underlying plan out of which the universe is constructed. It is the intention of the present voyage to disclose the underlying plan by means of a practical metaphysics.

The electron, once considered to be the smallest known particle of matter, moves around the nucleus of the atom in an elliptical orbit and has a lower energy interaction than do the particles within the core of the atom itself. Occasionally one skips an orbit under impact or pressure, and whenever it does it creates electro-magnetic waves of varying frequencies. Gamma rays have the highest frequencies, while radio waves are among the waves which have the lowest frequencies in the electro-magnetic spectrum. As far as can be determined, light waves circle the entire circumference of the universe at the uniform rate of 186,000 miles per second; this will later in our voyage lead us to postulate that all particles and waves are finally absorbed into a patternless stream of motion and it will become the basis for a theory of unreality.

Most cosmogonists do not believe there is any new basic primordial substance being created in the universe today; an examination into the relationship of the elements has led most of them to believe that there existed a primordial state before the elements were formed. They reason that the elements could only have been formed under conditions of immense gravity, intense heat and high vaporization whereby they could form aggregates of heavy matter. Many physicists speculate that in the center of the sun there may only exist sub-atomic particles like the protons and the neutrons; on the surface, however, where the temperature is several millions degrees cooler, hydrogen can be observed in the process of being transformed into helium.

Photographs taken with the most powerful telescopes reveal that the heavens are filled with countless flaming objects which have varying sizes and shapes. Some are so far away from us that it has taken their light several hundred million years to reach the earth's surface, and the light from some of the distant quasars may have started their journey two billion years ago. The speed by which many of the bodies are moving away from our own galaxy has led many a cosmogonist to believe that some high tension center set the universal system in motion. A few are apparently still trying to rid themselves of internal stress as they belch new stars out of the centers of their commotion; most of the galactic bodies, however, seem to be trying to stabilize themselves around some common center of gravity. The universe in general points to a state of decay and possibly to an ultimate death as the light from distant bodies varies from blue to red. There is evidence of elemental exhaustion in the red dwarf stars of the Milky Way, and even our own sun shows signs of exhaustion—we can watch it slowly depleting its energy resources by observing the thermo-nuclear activity at its surface. The earth, together with her sister planets, through their wide orbiting, varying revolutions, and shifting axes, tell the history of their once tempestuous origin and indicate that they are now slowing down and coming to a halt. Further confirmation of the solar-system's long history can be found in the rock stratification of the earth's surface, for it must have taken several billion years to transform all the elements and compounds into the many different kinds of rocks that go to make up the earth's geological structure. It is not known at present whether the solar system was laid down "hot" or "cold"; in the latter case there would probably have been a second breaking up of the universe, at least in part.

The above facts have led to the theory that the universe could have started as a giant atom which later exploded or puffed out as a giant galaxy, which in turn splintered into more than a billion galaxies and finally into more than a billion billion stars. Whether we consider the universe as a macrocosm or a microcosm, there is evidence that it started from a common center of tension: the universe and the elements are in a continual regression; the more concentrated their mass is, the greater their energy is and the more necessary it is to relieve their tension. The world is an expansion of particles and waves which comprise its mass and movement; which is always attempting to balance itself in stages that afford temporary relief but are never permanently able to endure. After the initial explosion, the tempo of the universe was set at the beginning and its pattern was manifested in the varying wholes of its reality, for it was necessary to resolve the tension in everything large as well as everything small. As the unstable wholes vary from the infinitely large to the infinitely small, they seek equalization in a final whole of stability, which will mean the end of the process.

CHAPTER IV

The Practical Pattern That Governs the Reality of the Universe

THE WORLD is a macrocosm, a world that is infinitely large; it is also a microcosm, a world that is infinitely small; and the poles of its movement lie between them. The inter-play and the intra-play of the infinitely large and the infinitely small movements of the system create temporary balances or wholes that constitute the reality of the universe. Every movement is caused by the movement of something else, every particle and every wave is displaced in the direction of a better balance—something more normal and complete. The universe is continually ridding itself of its lack of balance and is in process back to something more stable, and since it is in flux, it is moving all reality along with it. It does not matter how fragmentary and incomplete the stages and phases appear to be, they are relative to other stages and phases which go to make up the physical and scientific objects of the universe that are always on the move as the pattern that governs all things reduces the complexity of the reality movement. The movement of the universe is evolutionary because it follows a fixed pattern of escapes, reliefs and creations.

The billion billion stars and the substance of which they are composed are but tension stages that are governed by the escape-relief-creation pattern which was primordial with the creation of the universe, and the different stages of reality are seeking relief from what evidently has been an irrational beginning. The flight from chaos is manifested throughout all stages and phases of lessening tension as the very complex stages try to stabilize themselves in various formations and displacements. We live in a world which has attained some relief from the pent-up energy that was caused by the disruption of some high tension center and by means of which the universe is continuing to displace itself from one creative stage to that of another in search of further relief; an almost infinite number of protons, neutrons and electrons with an almost infinite number of combinations—the heavens are on fire and burning up before our eyes as they search for a final relief by means of a systematic evolution of lessening wholes of reality as the primal pattern weaves in and out on its long journey to eternity.

There is evidence of the escape-relief-creation pattern in the primal build-up of the elements; the escape-relief-creation of a single proton and electron comprises the basis for more than one hundred elements that make up the periodic table. The hydrogen atom is regarded as the primary one, the other elements being the multiples of the single proton and electron which form that element. Deuterium and tritium are steps in the formation of the heavier elements and are not found in a free state; lighter elements like hydrogen and helium comprise the largest percentage of all matter, while heavier elements like uranium are comparatively rare. We find that in the uranium series of elements the above process is reversing itself and the series is tearing itself down; inactive elements are regarded merely as ashes of once-raging nuclear fires. Both the building up and the tearing down of the elements are a part of the expanding and curving out of the universal reality, and for that reason we must regard space as positive. During our journey we shall assume that each reality-whole of the universe must find an escape, followed by a varying period of relief which results in a new creation stage of lessening tension until all wholes are completely absorbed into a patternless stream of motion.

Perhaps the uranium series of elements will afford the voyager the best example of the practical sequence of the escape-relief-creation pattern during the flight as it constructs the reality elements out of its stages and phases of lessening tension; each new element formed out of the previous one is a distinct reality in itself but is under pressure for a complete relief, and as it regressively accomplishes the task it slowly disintegrates and is transformed into a new reality element which has a smaller mass with less energy until the series is completed. Uranium has the greatest mass and greatest energy; radioactive lead has the least and is the end of the series. The slow displacement of the series enables the physicist to calculate the probable age of the solar system and the earth with a considerable degree of accuracy. Each whole or real element takes a measurable length of time before it is transformed into another element of the series, and the total of all the series adds up to almost five billion years, which is the estimated age of the sun and the planetary systems. However, it will take many times longer before all activity ceases and the system ends its span of existence.

Such a condition implies a negative movement since the universe can only find relief by tearing down stage after stage, and for this reason many of the physical phenomena appear irrational in ordinary terms of thinking, as each succeeding stage is constantly being dominated by a negated factor. However, there are two movements going on at the same time; while the universe as a whole is gradually achieving an ultimate balance, each reality-whole contains both a plus and a minus factor which is momentarily trying to balance itself. Due to the convergence of pressures of which the infinitely large and the infinitely small consist, it is the tendency of the various phases of activity to bind themselves into larger phases, where they inter-lock, or unite, and resist further change of motion; these stages become the reality-wholes of the universe. We find a pressure for stabilization in all universal fields of activity; the unseen force that is inherent in all physical bodies that we call gravity, and the plus and minus that binds all objects together, are powerful manifestations of material bodies the stabilization of which is displayed throughout the stages of cosmic evolution as the destructive movement continues to negate itself.

26

The heavens are filled with a host of flaming objects that are seeking to maintain a balance by means of gravity; every quantum of energy maintains at least a fleeting relationship with a more stabilized form of matter—pressures, stresses, etc., becomes waves of infinite wholes which comprise the reality movement that is seeking an ultimate completion. The balances, however, that make up the reality-wholes of the universe are merely preferred states of motion and the existence of such states makes it possible to separate a four-dimensional world of events into a three-dimensional space and a one-dimensional time. Therefore, mass is only a symbol of resistance to change of the forces behind the universe and is the result of the jamming of high-energy particles. All stages of lessening tension are only major phases of lessening tension, where mass is the interference through physical processes as the entire reality movement continues to negate itself in search of a final completion. A positive charge is never found free and is always associated with mass; when free it tries to balance itself out as far as possible. In a complexity of stages and phases, all things are continually on the move as they join all other things in a common flight from tension; the destructive process becomes the universal reality which is the sum total of all the adjustments in the tension centers which are displacing themselves towards the normal and the complete as the system expands and thins out and the process becomes more equalized. Thus the physicist is quite right when he states that the more he delves into the ultimate nature of reality the more wave-like it becomes, because matter is forever negating itself through stages and phases of lessening tension. The conception of the infinitely large and the infinitely small wholes of reality comprises a constant process of reduction, and their classification and systematization become the processes of knowledge wherein we use many letters and numerals to represent very complex realities. Nothing in the universe, however, has any fixed point, and things continue in varying degrees of flux as series of incompletions. Our very lives are processed out of a dynamic and fleeting reality.

Regardless of whether we think of the universe as in the direction of an ultimate negation or whether we think of it as a stabilized system of repetitions, the fleeing nebulae, the wheeling galaxies with their star systems, are in varying degrees of formation and decay throughout space as they escape from tension, winding and winding as they go in search of a greater stability. There is a reciprocal adjustment in every stage of their movement as their action and reaction play between the poles of their movement. The blind irrationality of the beginning can only find temporary relief from pressure through the fleeting wholes or balances we call reality as they slow down the movement and thus prevent a sudden completion of the various stages and phases of their activity. Despite a processed reality of diverse wholes, the pressure continues relentlessly onward towards eternity as the movement displaces itself in the direction of a final death. To the unthinking universe, the cause-space-time continuum is a part of the movement towards a final completion; absolute reality it will never know, nor is it concerned with human speculation.

Objects follow each other in sequences of varying wholes. We call these round, square, proportionate and symmetrical, etc., because it is practical to do so and they are the reals or norms of a process, as far as we are able to determine by their relationship. Science perseveres in its effort to classify and systematize the conception of wholeness and unity through laws that include a more complete conception of reality; the result is that many complex forms of matter have been reduced to their basic molecules and atoms. Since the physicist has formulated mass and equated it to energy, matter has been regarded as a very fluid conception; the greater the mass, the greater the energy as it is displaced from higher forms of energy to lower forms, from the positive to the negative, from the plus to the minus. All matter implies a transformation, and as it is being transformed it is essentially a behavior. Electricity is a behavior, time and space are relative. Constantly shifting realities comprise all physical processes, and their laws and equations rest upon them; some, like those in quantum physics, require many decimals in computing their measurements.

CHAPTER V

A Theory of Reality

AS THE PHYSICIST probes more deeply into the primal and ultimate nature of the physical world, the more mysterious that world becomes; if he considers the neutrino, he finds only high-energy interactions which keep resolving themselves into plus and minus particles; then, if he turns to light rays, he finds that their frequencies vary from very high, like gamma rays, to very low, like radio and television waves. All elements appear to be exhausting their energy resources and their realities at the same time, and the physical world can no longer be explained as matter. It matters little, according to Heisenberg and Born, whether we regard the ultimate physical world as made up of particles or waves since everything is reducible in the final analysis to probabilities. All laws become more difficult to formulate as the theoretical physicist nears the end of the process for the plus and minus; the positive and the negative become more equalized and the cause-time-space continuum draws near to its end. It is evident that a theory of reality which relies entirely upon the physical processes for its explanation can never fully explain the beginning and the ending of a material world. The solution to the primal and to the ultimate nature of the physical world must be sought in a bolder conception of reality.

The objection to any theory of reality that concerns itself solely with the physical world lies not so much in the physicist's failure to find the primordial substance of which all matter is composed but in his inability to complete the picture of a physical reality. The physicist's world is a splintered world, a world of vanishing realities which keep negating themselves into emptiness. Since the factors of physical reality are only splinters that can never be completely formulated, certain questions arise which press the theoretician for an answer. Is there a basic principle which underlies the reality of the universe and which governs its movement to a completion? Is the energy that is behind every physical process an exclusive property of the universe? What lies beyond space? Generally, the physicist evades the above questions by stating that the conception of the universe is still incomplete and the answers to such questions will have to wait until a better understanding of its fundamental nature can be had. This hope is held out to the inquisitive mind despite all past failures to explain the universe entirely in terms of a physical reality; thus, man waits and spends his whole life in a world of reality, finally stepping off its dark brink into oblivion without understanding its fundamental nature.

The reality of the known world is a processed and displaced one; out of the displacement there arises the universe—a vast system which stretches to eternity. Beyond the universe words fail us because they, too, are a part of the process. Words like God, spirit and being carry qualifications that are meaningful only to a world of which they are a part. Schelling believed that a word should carry no qualifications if it is to define or embrace the whole of reality, and the nearest that he could come to such a definition is the word "indifference." However, the ultimate or hypothetical completion of the process is essential if a conception of reality is to be of any practical consequence to the theoretician, otherwise the process will remain forever unresolved and the reality movement will always be processing the mysterious and the unknown. A final completion of the universe is difficult to conceive due to the great diversity and complexity of stages which exist throughout the movement; each whole of the movement is a reduction from the previous whole and each is a creation of destruction as the reality maintains its general direction towards some balanced condition which is a negation.

The basis for the conception of reality lies in a balanced

and unsplintered unit; all the wholes of reality must be constructed out of that unit, so that each whole of the process will be both the in-balance and the out-balance, by means of which a practical pattern can be developed until the movement is completed. The conception of such a unit would imply both a symbol of change and a symbol of changelessness before it is sprung out of balance by the distortion of the uniphase. Out of the disruption must come the pattern for the universe that governs the release of all tension until the end of the process is reached. Therefore, when I hereafter speak of the unit-of-the-cosmic I shall mean the unsplintered balance of the absolutely stable and unstable, the plus and minus, the gravity and inertia of whatever the unreality of the universe consists; this is as far as I can go in describing the unit, which is unreal and purely creative and which has no pattern to create a reality until it is distorted and splintered. And may I again state that it is not my intention to take the fire which I have stolen from the altars of science and use it to draw an impossible blueprint of the universe; the unit is not offered as a final conception of all the complex stages of the universe but is only projected hypothetically in order to separate a patterned reality from a nonpatterned unreality and thereby light our way to eternity by means of a practical metaphysics.

The physicist's conception of the universe as a vast and transformative process of greater mass and energy to lesser mass and energy makes it necessary to think of the universe as a continuous process if energy is the only indestructible thing in the universe; but a stabilized theory of the universe would have to rest on the assumption of a final and irreducible unit on the order of the neutrino, which is normally free from pressure but can abnormally be constructed or splintered into other units which in turn can be resolved back to a normal state. However, to do so, an escape would have to be effected and a relief attained in successive stages of creation with the infinitely large and small wholes of reality which make up the physical processes that are always seeking a balance. The process would also require a purely creative pre-conditioning phase before the advent of the giant atom, which would set the stage for the series of universal escapes, reliefs and creations that constitute the governing norm of the plus and minus factors of which mass and energy consist. Somehow, out of the plus and minus balances and the pattern, the known world of ours was created.

The cosmogonist maintains that in order to piece together a picture of the universe he must first start with a purely creative phase; but he is unable to find a purely creative phase in the universe. In charting the course of the universe, a complete outline of the process can be visualized by the postulation of a purely creative build-up of a pre-cosmic phase that is the unreality of a patternless stream of motion which contains the factor of "resistance to change" that is implied in all curvatures but as a part of unreality it is a variable negation. As a variable, the negated stream might be imagined as eventually becoming the un-splintered plus and minus balance of the unit-of-the-cosmic, which is further distorted and disrupted into the escape-relief-creation pattern of a splintered universal reality. After the pattern was created, it remained to become the governor or modulator which releases all the pent-up energy of every balanced whole of reality of the universe, which, as a processed reality, must still obey the indestructible law of resistance to change of motion throughout every stage and phase of lessening tension until all plus and minus balances are again absorbed into the patternless stream of motion. Due to the absorption of the universal reality into a patternless stream of motion, the cycle could possibly repeat itself through another pre-cosmic phase.

After the disruption of the unit-of-the-cosmic through the distortion of the inverted curvature, the unreality phase ended and reality began with the creation of the escape-relief-creation pattern. The processed reality includes the giant atom that created the components of the elements and then puffed out the giant galaxy and the subsequent varying wholes and decreasing stages of lessening tension—components that make up the complex movement of the universe

that is now seeking completion as represented in the geometrical series:

$$1 — \tfrac{1}{2} — \tfrac{1}{4} — \tfrac{1}{8} — 1/16 \ldots \ldots 0$$

Where 1 represents the giant atom, the diminishing fractions of the series represent the decreasing wholes of reality, and 0 represents the end of the series. A cause-time-
space continuum is set in motion by the escape-relief-creation pattern at the highest distortion point of the uniphase,
and it modulates the release of energy of all the splintered
particles and waves. There is an escape-relief-creation pattern in every reality-whole of the universe as the series
approaches the theoretical 0. It is quite clear that the 0
here represents infinity and that the process will never end
but will keep expanding in order to rid itself of the last iota
of tension.

If there is any satisfactory conclusion to the series it
will be necessary that the 0 represent the irreducible minimum. So instead of pyramiding the series of diminishing
fractions endlessly, suppose we substitute the letter N for
the 0, let it become the negation of a patternless stream of
motion, and allow it to become a completed condition of
the series. The N will become the theoretical goal of all the
fractions of the series, and all fractions both large and
small will end at N; and by imagining the 1 and the diminishing fractions as the reality-wholes of the universe they
will no longer exist as an extension of the universal reality,
and their cause-time-space continuum will be absorbed in
the negation. N as the patternless stream of motion would
forever cease to be the cause of future universal disturbances if it was not forced to obey the factor in all balances
—the law of the resistance to change of motion or curvature, the indestructible factor of both reality and unreality.
When expanding the curvature would form realities and be
positive; inverted it would contract, form an unreality, and
be negative or neutral. Here, in a purely creative phase, we
meet for the first time anti-space and the answer to the age-
old question of what lies beyond space.

A basic unit of matter has often been postulated by the physicist and conceived on the order of a neutrino or a photon, and a series of universes have been described as from neutrinos to neutrinos; but such a unit and like series of universes are definite realities as far as the physicist is concerned. The unit-of-the-cosmic as postulated in the foregoing is not a reality but an unreality—a plus and minus, or a gravity and inertia balance of a purely creative phase of motion that was formed by the inverted curvature which conceivably lost its pattern as some last line of tension. What the physicist does is to confuse the universal downward movement of a destructive reality with the purely creative build-up of an uniphase; a neutrino, since it is a part of the destructive process of the universe, must by necessity be a part of its reality-wholes. The physicist finds that this is true, for it starts an energetic process of bodies and antibodies. The separation of the patterned stream of the universal processes of reality from the nonpatterned stream of the uniphase is represented as a capsule in Figure 1. The answer to the question of whether the universe folds back or folds under is answered in the negative in both instances as the whole process is finally absorbed into the negation of a patternless stream of motion.

The difference between the unit sought after by the physicist and the one postulated as a plus and minus balance of a purely creative phase of negated motion lies in the latter's theoretical value of uniting a patterned world of reality with a non-patterned world of unreality that obeys the same law of resistance to change inherent in all forces and is therefore applicable to the known world of processes and the unknowable world of nonprocesses. For here the seed of all unifying laws lies latent in a patternless stream of negated and unrestricted motion until slowed by the contracted and inverted curvature and jammed into the unsplintered plus and minus, or gravity and inertia balance, later to be disrupted and sprung out of balance by its distortion into an escape-relief-creation pattern of the splintered high energy particles which created the giant universal atom and all the galactic systems. In a system which grows more extended and negated as the universal process is completed, the physicist can never hope to explain the physical reality solely in terms of fleeting particles and waves; he is only chasing the will-o'-the-wisp with little hope of ever catching its randomness, and subsequently he need never expect to construct a complete picture of the universe.

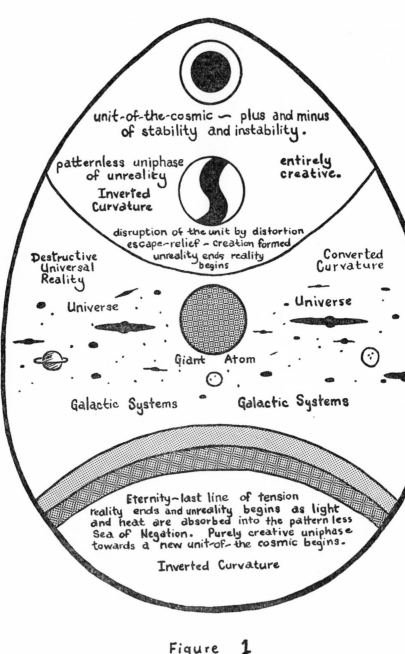

Figure **1**

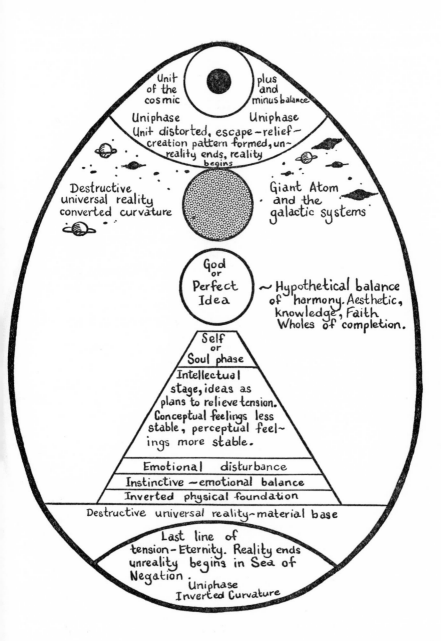

Figure 2

CHAPTER VI

Possible Adjustments of Science to a Theory of Reality

ALBERT EINSTEIN was successful in his endeavor to equate mass to energy and gravity to inertia but was not successful in his effort to unify the electromagnetic and the gravitational fields. As a physicist he sought to formulate a unified field in a world of diminishing realities where the net result is a law of no returns; the physicist's world is not a world that is building up, or a reversible reality, but a doomed world of an ultimate negation, and there is no formula that he can devise which will afford a satisfactory solution to any physical conception of a unified universe. It is as if someone had stood on a high precipice that overlooked a large and imperceptibly moving stream of water and pushed a huge boulder into it, causing an almost endless succession of decreasing waves until, finally, the last ripple was absorbed into the stream and its waves of reality were no more. Herbert Spencer considered energy as the only indestructible thing in the universe, but thought it to be in a continuous state of redistribution; from this assumption he deduced his famous law on the conservation of energy, but it was not believed at that time that the universe was in a state of decay. If the physicist could restrict all energy to the universe, as did Spencer, he might dispense with an ultimate negation altogether; but such an assumption is not in conformity with a complete picture of the universal reality, because the other half is missing.

The solution to the theory of reality must be sought in a patternless stream of motion, and from it must follow the explanation of the world as stages and phases of lessening tension which is governed by a practical escape-relief-creation pattern to a conclusion. When all matter is finally equated to energy or force there exist three states: the energy of the universe is restricted and splintered; the force of the negation is unrestricted; and the force of the unreal unit is restricted and unsplintered. It would be more consistent if the physicist would regard all the physical processes as restricted balances seeking an ultimate completion. This would be true whether they were particles or waves. Since gravity equates itself to inertia and matter thins out as space is extended, the elastic condition which surrounds a body would determine its physical properties. Quantum physics holds that the active physical processes consist of discrete particles of energy—indeed, the science of electronics is based upon this. Should not, then, some high-energy particle like the neutrino be regarded as the primary splintered unit and the beginning of the process, and the photon near the end, since many of the physical laws are also based upon the wave theory? This would lead to the hypothesis that all matter is eventually absorbed into a patternless stream of motion. In its primal and uninterrupted state, the neutrino is almost patternless but is powerfully energetic; its pattern only becomes discernible when it strikes other particles and begins a systematic process of escape, relief and creation. Light, with the speed of 186,000 miles per second, is a hampered motion of the electromagnetic spectrum; its pattern is much in evidence, since the varying wavelengths are modulated by an escape-relief-creation pattern like all restricted splintered forces of the universe which compose matter. At this point matter is being transformed into less restricted forms of energy, which are finally absorbed as heat by the patternless stream of motion. Gamma rays, with their high frequencies, represent the greatest resistance to absorption and are not available as sense data, while the longer visible light rays which offer less resistance to absorption are readily available as sense data. Still longer waves, like radio waves, need amplification before they can be used as sense data. Light waves travel at the rate of 186,000 miles per second; they have to, because that is the rate of the absorption base, or the patternless stream of motion, and the varying wavelengths represent their resistance to absorption. The idea that all energy is ultimately absorbed into a common medium is not new to the physicist, for it has often been theorized that all the energy of the universe will some day be converted into heat and the heat evenly distributed over the universe. If force is all that is left after every form of matter is resolved into its last indivisible components, we may assume that it is never destroyed, only that it loses the pattern by which we recognize it in the physical processes. After its absorption into the patternless stream of motion, it is least restricted at the last line of tension (eternity) and most restricted at the highest phase of its inverted curvature, where it becomes the unsplintered unit-of-the-cosmic to be later splintered by distortion into the escape-relief-creation pattern of the universal reality. The inverted curvature and the expanding curvature which comprise the unreality and the reality in Figure 1 might be compared to the elliptical and more-or-less restricted movement of the moon around the earth; being most restricted at its perigee and least restricted at its apogee. As we know energy in the universe, it is a negation of pluses in the unreality phase, it is the jamming of a negation.

While it would be impossible to formulate a law of unified fields for the universe in terms of a process, it would be possible to do so through a conception of a variable negation. To state that the variable negation has a speed dependent upon its resistance to change after absorbing all bodies and anti-bodies of the universe is consistent with the more advanced theories concerning the nature of a physical reality. A theory of reality, in the final analysis, would, therefore, come to rest upon a pre-cosmic or uniphase which obeys the same law of resistance to change as does that of a processed reality; however, such an assumption would imply that energy could be converted into matter. The feasibility of an anti-proton and an anti-neutron has already been demonstrated, and out of it has arisen the speculation that a situation might exist somewhere in the universe whereby the core of the atom could be reversed. The objection to the theory lies in the possibility that the positive and the negative atoms would cause a universal detonation unless the negative atoms could exist somewhere in the outer fringes of space by themselves.

As a part of the metaphysical framework of the universe, the resistance to the change of force or motion becomes a carry-over into the unreality phase and is a part of the combined capsule. As such it is the super-imposition of an inverted curvature of motion upon a converted curvature and is the law which ties the world of reality to the phase of unreality. As a part of the combined capsule of reality and unreality, the resistance to change of motion is comparable to the motion of a swiftly moving body of water when it reaches the U bend of a river, at which point it forms a vortex—the inner core of the body remaining relatively calm and representing the plus, and the outer-rim still moving violently and representing the minus. In this condition we can imagine we have a momentary state of balance of stability and instability, or a plus or minus, or gravity and inertia which we can postulate as the unit-of-the-cosmic. We might be further tempted to compare the jamming of the patternless stream of negation with that which takes place when a water molecule is modulated by the lowering or raising of its heat co-efficient, resulting in three distinct realities—ice, water and vapor. But there is no relief in sight for the unreality stream until it is balanced, distorted and splintered into the escape-relief-creation pattern and the high-energy particles of the universe.

One of the older theories that has been abandoned by the physicist is the belief that there exists a hypothetical substance called ether which fills all space and upon which all physical bodies float; by means of its undulations light travels from one end of the universe to the other. After the Michelson-Morley experiment this theory was held unlikely; the experiment proved there is no ground for the belief that there exists a substance such as ether. Perhaps the fault here again is in the conception of the physical reality and the sub-stratum which overlies or underlies its base, whether it is a substance or is motion. A patternless stream of motion would well substitute for the older theory provided the physicist keeps in mind that the unreality stream is the absorbent of the reality stream rather than a movement of a pattern which is seeking a haven through stages and phases of lessening tension in the universe. When the physicist thinks of an object he insists upon giving it a pattern of form, and when it runs out he has only the abstract, which is patternless. A patternless stream of motion cannot have a form, because it does not consist of an escape-relief-creation pattern, and without that all knowledge is invalidated. Neither can a purely creative phase rise from a patterned stream if it is intended in some manner to create the pattern of reality.

CHAPTER VII

Summary to Part One

THE OUTLINE presented for our voyage comprises a complete metaphysical framework for the conception of the universal reality after an unreality stream is balanced, then distorted and disrupted from the unknowable and patternless world. It is by means of this that we are able to vouchsafe a knowable and patterned world of reality which is continually negating itself and must continue to do so until all plus and minus factors are resolved at the last line of tension, which we call eternity. Here the process ends with the complete dissolution of the universe, and all of its energy is, again, absorbed into the patternless and unreal world of the unknowable. The solution to the problem of whether the universe is monistic or pluralistic is solved by placing the unsplintered unit-of-the-cosmic outside of the universal framework of reality movements and making the goal of the universe a variable negation, which is as normal a state as we can imagine. As long as the universe is displacing itself through stages and phases of lessening tension the contents of which are both stable and unstable, it is pluralistic; in so far as it accomplishes its goal to a more normal balance, it is monistic.

By picturing the universal Flight From Tension and separating a patterned world of diminishing realities—the world of the knowable—from a nonpatterned world of the unknowable—an unreal world which is purely creative—a broader outline of the universe has been presented which would not have been possible in a system of thinking that has as its content an Absolute Logos or consists of a *mysterious force*. The rationalism of Hegel is compelled by its law of inconsistency to guarantee forever a higher content wherein all differences can be reconciled; the Spencerian conception of reality restricts itself to the universe and can never satisfy the longing of the mind to know the why, the how and the whereto of things. A metaphysical framework, if it is to be of any practical benefit to the theoretician, must be the complete outline of a reality vehicle, with its many complex moving parts, which constitutes the balances or wholes of the universe and which obeys the same law of resistance to change as an unreality as it does as a reality. As an unreality, it is a cold god of an over-world of negation whose inevitable fate is an inverted curvature of motion whereby an unsplintered unit is created, unbalanced and splintered into the escape-relief-creation pattern of the universe. After the creation of the escape-relief-creation pattern, the world of unreality ended and the pattern took over the task of resolving all the splintered wholes of the universe, with its bodies and anti-bodies, that were formed by the omnipresent law of resistance to change as the pattern continued to modulate the release of all the pent-up energy of the universe in stages and phases of lessening tension. But the pattern necessarily had to precede the formation of the universe and be co-extensive with its displacement; it is, therefore, a part of the cosmic urge to reach an inevitable conclusion of the process. The pattern is essentially a system of reduction from one stage of higher tension to that of a lower one and it is always sufficiently complementary to follow in sequences of escapes, reliefs and creations. However, it never effects an entire escape, or a full relief, or a full creation; but it comprises the governing norm of all the destructive forces of the universe and is found wherever there is universal activity.

That such a practical pattern exists is evident in the creation of the elements. It is found in the periodic tables, and in the tearing down of the elements, as in the uranium series; it is also found in the expanding star systems, starting from a high-tension center like a giant atom and then evolving into countless tension centers of varying complexities. Each stage of lessening tension is a new creation, but it must always contend with the positive and the negative of the succeeding stage, which embraces a new reality-whole of lessening tension. Although not always apparent in the world of scientific objects like the neutrino, which can neither be seen nor felt, the pattern is successful in achieving a partial balance in the world of physical objects since they appear by means of sense impressions as stages or processes of knowledge. There is always a point of rest or balance, if for only an instant, which is relative to some other balance, although both are an insignificant part of the whole process and exist only as symbols or abstractions of the primal eruption that started the universe in search of completion. The stages or balances are roughly analogous to the stops or balances of a very intricate piece of machinery which has many different-size cog-wheels. Since there exists no perfect circle, for a circle is composed of many segments, a wheel must come momentarily to a halt when it meshes with another wheel as it continues to turn. By imagining the wheel segments as the resistance to change of motion of the universe, we may conclude that there are as many complex stages as there are balances possible in the universe as it journeys on its way to completion. All the fragments, stops and divisions of the universe consist of stages and phases out of which are created the diminishing wholes of reality that are seeking an ultimate balance; every stage is relative to some other stage that is seeking to momentarily balance itself, but is evolutionary with the whole of the process as the system is being displaced towards a final balance. Despite the irrational blindness of every stage, the goal of the universe is definite and conclusive—it is seeking a balance that will mean the end of the process of destruction. The escape-relief-creation pattern of the universe constitutes all we know of the Law of Consistency, and the stable and unstable factors behind the stages and phases of lessening tension comprise all there is to the necessity of continuance. Without the pattern, we would be faced with a very complex world indeed. By means of the pattern the world of objects is being gradually reduced to the minimum terms of their practicability, and by the modulation of the pattern a pluralistic world is being reduced to a monistic one. As science has done so, the progress to the conception of the world has been greatly increased; and paradoxically, through the reversal of the process of destruction by means of a constructive life process, we have achieved our greatest values in freedom.

Later, in Part II, we shall find that the reality of life is but an inversion of the reality of the universe and is the reversal of the destructive movement, for reality is now on the increase instead of on the decrease. Both, however, will comprise an evolutionary movement as the rational processes of life and the irrational processes of the universe are set against each other until all conflict between their inbalances and out-balances are resolved by means of a practical escape-relief-creation pattern. While the irrational universe is tearing down reality after reality, the rational life process will be building a constructive world of experience and be counter-pointing it to the destructive metaphysical stream by the pyramiding of harmonies as it seeks a positive conclusion in a hypothetical balance which, if possible of attainment, would constitute the fourth metaphysical stage of life. Since, however, the biological reality is a patterned one, like that of the universe, it must confine itself to the irrational universe. Its ultimate fate, then, is contingent upon that of the universe.

Perhaps the only satisfactory relationship which can exist between a destructive and a constructive process of reality consists in placing the "cold unit" outside of the universal framework and permitting the "warm biological unit" to remain within it. The universe is continually tearing itself down and has as its goal an ultimate negation; the life process is constantly building itself up and has as its goal a hypothetical balance of harmony, and must therefore remain forever a real movement. Life starts from the negative pole of its movement and is a nothingness until it is negated by another life movement. Thus, life starts as a constructive negation and must search for its completion in an ideal realm; therefore, it is basically an ideal or spiritual movement. Knowledge, if it is to be valid for both

46

movements, must be the moderator for both the universe and life as they attempt to resolve their differences and complete their movements. Objects which belong to the world of experience are processes of knowledge that are constructive and comprise a built-in process of reasoning which is governed by a practical escape-relief-creation pattern valid for both the movement of life and the movement of the universe. Therefore, a common pattern ties the two worlds together.

The diversity of tensions which rise out of the plus and minus of the infinitely large and infinitely small wholes of reality constitute the variety wholes or balances of knowledge through processes of thinking. There are as many systems of thinking possible in the universe as there are complexities of stages and phases and phases and stages that are seeking an ultimate or hypothetical completion; knowledge, nevertheless, is always on the increase because it is part of the life process which is continually creating an experience complex. The science of knowledge consists of the reduction or construction of a complexity of stages and phases and phases and stages that are seeking an ultimate or hypothetical completion, and it must confine itself to the possibility of the universal and the biological reality. Symbols and abstractions of the world of science are no more than the interaction of the destructive forces of the universe and the constructive forces of life that are trying to balance themselves through the wholes of the life movement.

Part II

THE THREE METAPHYSICAL STAGES
OF LIFE

CHAPTER VIII

Preface to Part Two

A MAZE of secrets which were hidden by time still hide many facts concerning life from the prying eyes of the scientists who would like to delve more closely into life's mysteries, but the fact of its lowly origin was revealed by Charles Darwin in his *The Origin of Species,* published in 1859. Darwin, in his theory of evolution, was able to explain life as the development of higher and more complex forms from lower and more primitive ones; chance variations, the struggle for existence, the survival of the fittest, and the transmission of useful characteristics by the strongest, were factors in the evolution of life. There was no need any longer for the older theories such as vitalism and special faculties. Darwin soon won support for his theory from fellow scientists of his day who were quick to discover in the new theory how both life and the universe could now fall under the same broad classification of change, the same dialectical transformation, and the same philosophy of becoming.

Up to the time of Darwin a scientist who was trained in a specialized field often would refuse to cross over into another field of science, but the one hundred years since the publication of the Theory of Evolution has witnessed the narrowing of the gap which previously separated the different branches of the biological sciences. Today it would be difficult to catalogue the many contributions to the life sciences which have been made by combining the talents of specialists from widely separated fields of endeavor. By means of bio-chemistry, a new approach to the understanding of the life principle has been opened. One discovery reveals how a living organism is supplied the energy needed in its functioning. When an organism produces its energy it must do so by chemical means, because the life processes are very close to its material base at the physical stage. This is accomplished in living organisms by means of the ATP molecule (ATP is the abbreviation for the chemical compound known as adenosine triphosphate). The ATP molecule gets its boost from the element phosphorous, which is very unstable in its chemical relationship; its electrons are readily available to be shared with other compounds which are themselves unstable. By means of the ATP molecule the more unstable organic compounds are able to borrow an additional electron from the phosphorous compound; when they do, a fusion takes place and a new chemical bond is forged and energy is released. All the energy needed by a living organism for its functioning is produced by many such alliances.

There are many secrets of life being uncovered through better means of research; after the invention of the electron microscope the cell structures of living organisms were found to consist of minute organelles that were well diversified and able to maintain a consistent life pattern. The discovery of the DNA molecules was a revelation into the blueprinting of life by the genes, which are the hereditary factors that control all biological development and are transmitted by means of the chromosomes. The electron microscope has also aided the virologist in the investigation of the mosaic (tobacco) virus. This is a form of life so primitive that it may be regarded as half life and half chemical, since it can exist in a crystalline state for months without its life potency being affected; but when placed in a warm, nourishing solution, it suddenly takes on the form of life and starts reproducing its kind. Much has yet to be learned about the nature of this virus, but it is now known that the nucleic acid chain is most important in its functioning. The virus has no proper cell wall of its own but somehow is able to penetrate the wall or membrane of another cell; once inside it lives off the cell until the cell is completely destroyed. There are many types of virus which cause a variety of diseases, and it is believed that when an immunization can be found against them, most infectious diseases can be cured or prevented.

Diseases that are associated with aging, such as those of the heart, and cancer, confront medical science with its greatest challenge; but that the destructive universal pattern may play a decisive role probably has already been guessed by the voyager. As far as the science of medicine is concerned, the life pattern presents many problems in the quest for the cure of some of the more stubborn and difficult diseases. For example: At what stage do the life-sustaining rays of the sun turn into skin cancer; or under what conditions are X-rays useful in the retardation of the growth of cancer cells, and at what intensity do they speed their growth? At present the answers to these questions are difficult to ascertain. It could be that a discerning virologist will someday find the answer to the above questions in the nucleic chain of the lowly virus. Too, it may be that he will find the confirmation of the practical life pattern with which we shall presently be concerned in The Three Metaphysical Stages of Life. For as we have already pointed out, the physical sciences are not adequate in explaining the basic principle of the universe, and we can hardly expect the biological sciences alone to be capable of explaining the basic principle of life. Scientific progress is dependent upon trained specialists, and if training in a specialized field of knowledge was the only qualification necessary in explaining life and the universe, there are many well qualified for such a task; but mere training in a specialized field has never and will never fully explain the reality of life and the universe. For in the universal process, the whole is always less than the sum of its parts, and in the life process the whole is always more than the sum of its parts. When the physicist reduces complex matter from the molecule to the atom and from the atom to the electron he finds that matter is always negating itself; when the psychologist traces the course of the thinking process from stimuli to sensation and from sensation to feeling he finds that life is constructively negating itself. Scientific knowledge is a part of a world of symbols and abstractions that comprise a knowing world of superficial realities—the surface complexities of an irrational universe and a rational life process—and it is likely that the physicist and psychologist will have to enlarge upon their specialized worlds through the means of a practical metaphysics.

CHAPTER IX

Life as the Inverted Pattern of the Universe

WE ARE concerned on the first leg of our journey with The Flight From Tension, taking a cue from the cosmogonist, who claims that the universe might have been created out of a large tension center which had a dense concentration of high-energy particles—from this a patternless stream of motion was projected that consisted of the unreality of a variable negation. In charting the negation stream, it was theorized that it conformed to the motion of all curvatures —whether expanding or contracting—to the factor of inertia, or the resistance to change of motion, the law of both the real and the unreal. As the unreality stream continued onward it was forced to conform to this law and as a result it was jammed into an unsplintered plus and minus balance—the unit-of-the-cosmic. The unit remained purely creative as it had not yet acquired a pattern for a reality, but it was later disrupted by distortion into the escape-relief-creation pattern of the universe with its splintered particles and laws. After the universe was formed, the pattern continued to govern all the reality stages and phases of lessening tension but had to obey the indestructible law of resistance to change of motion as the movement continued to systematically negate itself.

The pattern first created the giant atom of the universe with its splintered plus and minus components and then began expanding the universal reality. We can observe the movement in the galaxies, and it is also evident in the decay of radioactive elements. As the universe releases itself from its restrictions and moves nearer to completion, the inter-play and the intra-play of the infinitely large and infinitely small wholes of reality create a diversity of pressures through which the process tries to maintain itself in stages, and if sufficiently long and durable they may become stages of knowledge. Another world of scientific objects, while we cannot experience it directly, is equally real and can be ascertained by scientific experimentation. The universe has completed, perhaps, more than ten billion years (dependent upon whether our solar system was laid down hot or cold five billion years ago) toward an ultimate negation. The Second Law of Thermodynamics furnishes us a means of estimating that which remains before all the energy of the universe is released from its mass and the reality process will have become exhausted and vanish at the last line of tension.

The theory of reality that was developed in The Flight From Tension has been carried a step further in The Three Metaphysical Stages of Life. The contention is that the will is the inverted pattern of the universe and, like it, is seeking an ultimate completion through balances or wholes of lessening tension; these wholes constitute the reality of the biological process, but like the balances of the universe they are never permanently able to endure. The phases and stages of life, however, are constructive and consist of harmonies that are adaptive and rational and are opposed to the balances of the universe, which are irrational and destructive. But it is the contention of The Flight that if there had never been an escape-relief-creation pattern there would have been neither life nor the universe. The perpetual conflict that ensues when the life movement is pitted against the movement of the universe involves a counterbalance by which the rationality of life is set against the destructiveness of the universe as the life process develops towards a hypothetical balance of harmonies through the evolution of finer balances. A restless universe keeps urging, constantly pressing, for a solution to its irrationality, and the will has been caught in the tempo of the search and forced to develop harmonies in order to survive.

As an inverted pattern, the will is like the converted

pattern of the universe in so far as both are seeking a complete relief from tension; but whereas the universe decreases in its reality, the reality of life increases. Both patterns constitute the Law of Consistency through escapes, reliefs and creations, and the stable and unstable factors behind each of the movements is the necessity of their continuance. Where the infinitely large and the infinitely small intermingle, they create the complex world in which we live, one that is universally in dissolution but ideally or spiritually under construction. The phase always precedes the stage in the process of life, for the will's emphasis on creativity is diametrically opposed to the universe's impulsion for destruction, which displays its irrationality by tearing down stage after stage. This distinction is important in helping to clarify the opposite direction of the movements; usually the failure to note the distinction is where much of the misunderstanding of their relationship lies. It is also well to remember that the word "dialectical" is used in The Three Metaphysical Stages of Life to denote the inevitableness of the development of life only so far as the means of freedom are available; it is somewhat different in meaning when applied to the universe.

During the early and turbulent history of the earth the environment was not suitable for the creation and maintenance of a constructive life process, and more than two billion years passed before the earth was suitable for its habitation. In the diversified and specialized activity of life, the process had to be especially favored. Life has completed more than two billion years in the effort to right its balances, as compared to the nearly five billion for that of earth. There are many who believe that life is a normal constituent of the universe since it is composed of the commonest elements, while there are others who believe that it might have started at some early period of the earth's cooling—a period that was propitious for the creation of a giant protein molecule which would be able to support a constructive chain of nucleic acids which, in turn, produced the necessary amino acids for the functioning of a living organism. Whatever conditions that were necessary for its creation and maintenance, ways had to be found to relieve the tensions of life through the pyramiding of harmonies which were directive throughout the increasing complexity of phases and stages, and means had to be found to pass the increments onto the next generation in minute and almost faithful detail.

Life began as a transitory stabilization phase and stage and commenced its struggle for existence out of the disintegrating stages and phases of the universe and continued to develop other phases and stages out of the shifting stages and phases of its irrationalism. As the universe shifts its stages, life is compelled to do likewise. The relief is analogous to that of the universe, as it must create a new stage that has less tension than that of the previous one. Should life be entirely successful in finding complete relief in any of its newly created stages, it would end its existence in the oblivion of stability. As a rule, inorganic compounds end in equations that are relatively stable for a short time at least but, due to their general destructive nature, they are not suitable for the building of a constructive life process where a more flexible organization is required. Life attained a higher degree of diversity and a better adaptability by reversing the universal pattern; it inverted the pattern but kept its sequence and commenced to weave cross-threads of harmony into the irrational stages of the universe. Through the use of the element carbon as a building block for organic compounds, the life processes became more and more intertwined with the physical processes of the universe.

The flight of the universe from tension through varying wholes of completion is the key to the understanding of life, for it has been intimately associated with the destructive process from its inception and, by necessity, has followed its stages and phases of lessening tension in the development of its own phases and stages of lessening tension. When we come to investigate the reality of life, we find that same physical world which locks in the universal framework also encases the developing stages of life. Life is beset with continual disintegration and, like the universe, is attempting to escape from tension as it strives for a balance of its stable and unstable factors—the same urgency for stability is common for both reality processes, and each maintains itself by balances for varying lengths of time. The fleeting pressure-wholes of the universe have become the inverted pressure-wholes of life and are no more than the folding in and out of the biological phases and stages by an escape-relief-creation pattern. There is no quantitative difference between body and matter, feeling and energy; matter and energy are the blind unthinking stuff of which everything is composed.

The created embodiments of existence are but temporary balancing stages with which life confronts the universe in its struggle for existence. The shifting stages and phases of the universe and the counterbalancing phases and stages of life are synonymous with the conception of wholeness and unity no matter how complex they may seem to be—the spark, the escape, the temporary balance, the relief, stability, the goal through creative stages, comprise all the range of facts that are open for investigation. Neither life nor the universe can ever attain complete relief because they can never deal in absolute motion and absolute rest. But the end is what each is seeking, one constructively and the other destructively. The in-between changes represent a progression for one and a regression for the other from their original starting point by the building up or the tearing down of stages that are evolutionary in their movement towards either a hypothetical balance or an ultimate absorption in a negation. Life is attempting to achieve a permanent form in the universe, which itself can never attain absolute permanency as a process but only in a negation which is not realizable. Later we shall see that life can idealize a complete balance of harmony, although it will never be able to entirely embrace it.

Life is hemmed in by an infinite number of tension centers with their unstable and moving points; the forces of the universe not only wage a war of annihilation against it but also become a blanket that wraps itself around all biological forms and encases them. Life must carry the blanket with it wherever it goes, and were it not for the divisions, differentiations and specializations that are the essential characteristics of its constructive movement, it would have been destroyed at its inception. The inconsistency of life with that of the universe is the rational effort of the will to survive as opposed to the irrational effort of the universe to destroy it. Life must take the mechanically destructive pattern of the universe and out of it build the spiritually constructive pattern of the will to survive; it is subject to all the irrationality of the universe as it creates its forms, movements and laws and makes them the foundation of its rationalism. The complexity of life, like that of the universe, is due to the diversity of its pressures and not to the consistent pattern that governs its movement toward stability.

CHAPTER X

The Rationality of Life Is Governed by the Category of Refinement

SCIENCE, as a classified and systematized body of knowledge, cannot find in a strictly materialistic interpretation of the universe any evidence for the existence of a supernatural being who directs its destiny; there is only a blind relationship between the stages and phases of lessening tension. Most of what we call orderliness, scientists tell us, is due to sufficient reasoning. The eye recognizes as visible light only a small band of frequencies in the electromagnetic spectrum, and our hearing and other senses are likewise restricted to their usefulness in the furthering of life in its struggle for existence. As far as science can ascertain, there was no rational cause for the disruption that set the universe in motion; nor is there any rational cause displayed in any of its manifestations—floods, hurricanes and volcanoes are too indifferent to human suffering in their havoc to be the work of an anthropomorphic being. All facts that can be gathered from a candid examination of nature support the theory that the operation of the physical world is mechanical and impersonal; a world in which everything joins every other thing in a common flight from tension as they continue on their way to eternity.

Both the physical stage of life and the material stage of the universe make contact at some point at the beginning or ending of their phases of lessening tension. In photosynthesis, the energy of the sun is converted and transformed into usable physical energy by the chlorophyll in the leaves of plants to begin the construction and maintenance of a plant organism. At the instinctive stage of animal organisms, sense data begin at a point where the will, the inverted pattern, reverses the destructive process of the universe and begins pyramiding the incoming material tension of the objective world of reality into its own constructive experience complex of lessening tension. Out of these constructive processes of sense impressions there arises the world of the worm, the world of the dog, the world of the savage and the world of civilized man, all representing different stages of a constructive development of a release from tension. As the material world of objects releases its electrons they become negations; in the intellectual stage of life, the emotional energy of an instinctive stage is freed and becomes feeling, another negation. Both the universal and the biological processes become more wave-like as they release themselves from restrictions in the final phases of freedom.

Life, however, is more than a "swish of cosmic tension," or a concatenation of stages; it is more than a bundle of adaptations with physical incasements; it is more than division, differentiation and specialization. Without the world of physical objects there would only be left a world of particles and waves that would be too fleeting for the life process to create its categories through. But life is more than an interconnection of sensory organs that receive sense data from an outside world of physical objects. It is true that life is constantly being swept onward by an irrational universe and that mass is just as necessary to prevent the sudden completion of the life processes as it is for the processes of the universe; however, it is to be remembered that the goals of the two movements are different. By inverting the cosmic pattern of irrationality but retaining its sequence, the will was able to assert its dominance over the destructive movement. Thus its irrationality ended, at least for the time being. As the universe grows colder, more negative and unreal, life grows warmer, more positive and real.

The movement of life is in constant opposition to the movement of the universe. In the course of time it was able to lessen the tensions in three metaphysical stages, namely, the physical, the instinctive and the intellectual, since it was constructively able to intensify the effort to survive through the enlargement and activity of an emotional phase which provided a larger freedom for its development. As animal organisms develop their emotional phases they have to be stabilized by the instinctive stage and corrected by a higher intellectual stage, and this constitutes the difference between the subjective, that which is, and the objective, that which is aimed at, or the habitual and the flexible. The activity of the different phases and stages fall under the general urge of the will for stability and must be refined as a categorical necessity. The emotional phase as well as the three metaphysical stages are intertwined by the same pattern, which is seeking an ultimate but nevertheless hypothetical completion. It is possible for life to complete itself by means of the physical, the instinctive-emotional and the intellectual-feeling stages of development, which furnishes the clue to the aim of life as a rational life process of lessening tension.

Both a diverse and a specialized creation of harmonies are involved in the evolution of life, and they are maintained by a framework of adaptations as the biologically real process projects itself against an irrationally real one. Life is an organism for refinement by refinement that is categorically selective as it constructs the harmonies of life; life must add value to value in order to survive. The will, as a category of refinement, constitutes a built-in process of reason at every stage of life, always working mechanically through the physical as it "superejects" itself by the metaphysical. It is for this reason that a protoplasmic cell which forms the physical basis for life is not a sufficient explanation for all biological stages; the life pattern always has more than a physical adaptation as its ultimate aim. It is the pyramiding of the harmonies that are constructed by means of a dialectical escape-relief-creation pattern that is directive of all three metaphysical stages of release which motivates the will to achieve a full balance of harmony and thereby complete itself. Thus the Darwinian theory of natural selection is not invalid but merely superseded by a natural law of refinement.

All stages of life must have a base in the physical processes that form their tissues and organs, but they must also have a higher phase of intensity before they become adaptations with physical encasements. Life at the highest pitch of intensification is experimental as it searches for the greatest amount of harmony that is consistent with the particular stage of its development; at the lowest physical stage the harmonies are grouped together in a variety of ways where they are more stable and where the higher stages of mobility can be built around them. The stages of life comprise a complex of refinements throughout all unicellular and multicellular tissues and organs and are harmonized by means of a network of communication lines and centralized directives. Thus, life may be regarded as a continual process of adjustments with an infinite amount of possibilities that are activated by the constant urging of the will for stability. The evolution of life as a complex of harmonies represents values gained by the freeing of the life processes from the universal and biological pressures; as life releases itself from a manifold of tensions it advances by its rationality a step higher in the fulfillment of its metaphysical aim.

The processes of life are a metaphysical stream which is seeking completion, and as it develops it systematically turns the evolutionary stream and constructive phases and stages against the destructive stages and phases of the universe and progresses towards a hypothetical balance of harmony. A blind will has taken all discordant elements that challenge its existence and moulded them into adaptations or wholes of harmonious balances which compose the reality movement to completion. Like the processes of the universe, there are two movements going on at the same time: one represents the biological law of resistance to change of motion—it is the most apparent, and the one of which we are the most aware; the other is metaphysical— it is the least apparent and is the one with which we shall be largely concerned on the present leg of our flight to eternity. In the development of their balances both life and the universe are basically freeing operations; the effort of the will at the physical and instinctive stages is blindly rational, but at the intellectual stage it is more self-activated and free due to a sustained phase of conscious reasoning.

Life has developed within a limited sphere of a stage of the universe, but under favorable climatic and terrestrial conditions it has not only been able to survive but has also been able to gradually increase in value by means of its divisions, specializations and diversifications. The specialization and diversification of life into orders, genera and species go to make up a numerous and complex variety of life forms with almost endless adaptations. If it is true that the mills of the gods grind slowly but exceedingly fine, then it is especially true of the processes of evolution; so painstaking and slow has the evolution of life been that many of its intricate functionings are not understood even to this day; each organ is a marvelous feat of unity and functioning. Medicine has long been fascinated by the efficiency and perfection of the respiratory, circulatory and nervous systems and by the masterful control of the latter by the most remarkable organ of them all, the highly specialized and differentiated mechanism of the brain.

CHAPTER XI

Life in Search of the Ideal Completion

THERE IS always a diversity of pressures both within and without an organism to frustrate the will's aim of completion; but that the movement is governed by a practical pattern is manifest even at the genetic level, and it is doubtful if any other rational explanation can be given for the persistence of the hereditary stream of life. During the early period of the Darwinian theory the term "continuity of the germ plasm" meant that as life undergoes its various cycles of development, it likewise undergoes all the previous stages of its evolution—from tadpole to frog, from frog to dog, from dog to ape and from ape to man—but the theory is not widely accepted by the embryologists of today. A more practical explanation of the continuity of the germ plasm is to be found in the escape-relief-creation pattern that monitors all the life processes from one generation to the next and from the species of one to that of another as the will becomes better organized as an instrument of refinement. For the will is not only interested in the individual but in the completion of the entire life movement as it endeavors to right its balances and prevent the metaphysical stream from becoming stagnant.

Variety in unity as a law of nature makes its appearance at the unicellular level of the life processes; colonies of microscopic organisms have frequently been observed to conjugate at intervals. It is believed by micro-biologists that they do so in order to exchange heterogeneous characteristics and thus prevent the stagnation or sterilization of the genetic stream. Higher in the development of life there are still extant birds that are nearly sterile among their own species but are often fertile with a more closely related species. In the latter case the genetic in-balance and out-balance is facilitated and the species is perpetuated by the out-breeding of the species. It would appear to the casual observer that unity through variety would be a contradiction of the theory that life as a process is seeking stability through balanced wholes of harmony, but it is to be remembered that variety is essential in the construction of harmonies which the life process must posit against a diverse and complex universe, and the ultimate goal of completion for each is in the far distant future. Whereas the movement of the universe is from complex systems to a state of dissolution, the life movement is from simpler forms to more complex ones and the pattern is the solution in resolving the differences.

As a sequence of escapes, reliefs and creations, the category of refinement is found working at all metaphysical stages of development. At the physical stage it is displayed in the flowering and fruiting of shrubs and trees; at the instinctive stage, where the process has increased its activity by means of a sustained phase, it is manifested in the songs and nesting of birds; and at the intellectual stage we find the movement has become more fluid and the conscious process is able to differentiate the emotions into ideal balances of finer feelings (contents of feeling) where they can be used to formulate higher freedom concepts. The pattern of life as an idealistic adventure must always operate from a physical base, but it also must always consist of an escape-relief-creation pattern that is seeking an ultimate completion. Life as a constructive process of metaphysical stages always recreates its idealism as if from a physiological computer, with its many complex binary systems of notation. Life's developing idealism has its foundation at the genetic level, where all past racial history is stored, later to be passed onto the next generation, the next generation being the new balanced whole of idealism.

In the chromosomes of an individual member of a species are the genes that monitor all hereditary factors of both the individual (ontogeny) as well as the race (phylogeny), through which they are perpetuated as they undergo the evolution of life amidst an ever-changing condition until they achieve the best possible adjustment. If progress is to continue, the next higher life stage must take over the task of completing the life stream through a higher degree of mobility in order to further the reality of life. At the genetic level, division is the escape; the relief is in differentiation, and the new creative stage is another life entity with a new series of specializations or adaptations. By virtue of the imperative for refinement, the accumulated realities of lesser wholes have become the realities of the larger wholes as the metaphysical stream keeps generating species after species with their diverse characteristics. Since the characteristics of the individual can be transmitted through inheritance, the life stream can potentially carry on to eternity provided life can be that rational.

The possibility of ontogenetic development lies within the soma cells that have developed out of the reproductive cells and which contain the genes and the determinates that regulate the development of a particular life cycle. It would be almost impossible to exhaust the varied characteristics of a human at conception when a sperm cell is fused with the ovum, which is destined to become the soma cells of a new life cycle. While the ontogenetic possibilities of a human at conception are almost unlimited due to the wide variety of its instinctive-emotional and intellectual-feeling development, the physical possibilities of many species have long become exhausted by being too highly specialized. This could have been one of the contributing factors in the extinction of the dinosaur, which ruled the ancient marshes for more than one hundred million years. But it is probable that the huge animal may have also become extinct due to insufficient out-breeding. For it is reasonable to suppose that as the marshes shrunk the habitat of the dinosaurs became restricted and, as a result, they became sterile. The same lack of a genetic in-balance and out-balance may have caused the huge sea serpents to disappear at the same time, because as the food became more plentiful in the seas, the serpents did not have to range as far and consequently they became sterile and extinct.

The will was the incarnation of restlessness from the beginning, for the universe kept closing in on it at every turn. Being blindly rational, it would tolerate no "darlings"; those who could not win in its ceaseless combats went down in agony. At times it seemed to glory in the grotesque and fiendish monsters it created, and delighted in the instruments it devised for torture. Most of its creations it wantonly destroyed, others reached the dead-end of their development and could advance no further. The persistence in the natural law of refinement produced wide differentiation and caused intensive specialization until many of the species became well adapted to their surroundings. Life under such circumstances became fixed, as some orders and species found that they could meet the challenges to their existence within a close confinement or makeshift haven of stability. As a result of this, the metaphysical stream of many orders and species became greatly restricted and remained largely unchanged for millions of years, as was the case with the ancient progenitors of the present day crayfish. While many of the species were quite successful in their search for stability, others were forced to make constant adjustments to a diversity of pressures through means of new adaptations or ideas, and whenever this occurred it furthered the metaphysical aim of life. Subsequently the metaphysical stream continued to flow towards a greater physical, emotional and intellectual freedom. Since the impulsion behind the movement of life is a balance of harmony it became the basis of all rationality and the reason for being; and despite the apparent recklessness and utter futility of trying to achieve a balance of harmony in such an irrational world, the life process continued to make slow progress towards a hypothetical balance. The urge to escape from the tensions of life was so great that the movement gradually developed into higher phases and stages of lessening tension as the will systematically released itself from the irrationality of the universe and the blind rationality of the lower stages.

As it did, it continued to progress towards an ideal balance or a spiritual whole of completion.

The constant struggle that persists everywhere there is life impresses on the mind the ruthlessness of a natural law whereby only the fittest have survived. For it is obvious that nature has built her values only through the strongest and handed them down to the next generation through the fittest. This inexorable law has produced an amazing variety and number of species which have as their immediate criterion the survival of the strongest member of the species; a relentless will has had to wrest its values from the irrational universe and pit its harmonies against it. Actually, however, the will chooses the brutal method out of necessity, for its prime concern is harmony, which it creates endlessly and which it posits against the destructiveness of the universe in order that the tensions of life might be lessened and the ideal balance of harmony furthered towards a hypothetical completion. Wherever it has been possible for the will to do so it has fashioned its harmonies into unity, symmetry and proportion, making it possible for the pattern of form to develop from it; first, through means of a blind rationalization and later by means of a freer and more self-activated intellectual stage. Out of this highest metaphysical stage of life there eventually came all of the arts and sciences.

At first the will was content to let the life process develop pragmatically; the fragmentary reals of the universe were a challenge to its survival. They developed by necessity into balanced wholes of harmony, and as they evolved they became more complete and provided categories by which could be measured their experience and which could be used for future reference. Each adjustment, repeated a sufficient number of times, became an adaptation which again had to be refined in order to further a biological reality of greater wholeness. Thus, in the beginning, we find that the adaptations of life were of practical value. This was the result of the pattern's struggle with the immediate present; later, as ideal wholes, they became increasingly more fluid and directed the movement towards an idea or spiritual whole of completion. The word "ideal" is used in an inclusive sense to mean the entire life process regardless of whether it is blindly rational or consciously activated; and the word "spiritual" is used to mean a disembodied phase, or that which is hypothetical.

CHAPTER XII

Life as a Mind Pitch

IT IS NOT unusual for theologians and philosophers to express a belief in a dominant mind principle behind the movement of life, and there are many scientists who hold a similar view. Ernst Haeckel believed that every cell has a psyche and that life is the sum total of its psychic cells. After studying the life sciences for many years, Professor William McDougal of Duke University reached the conclusion that life is only the gradation of the mind. The mind, however, does not lend itself readily to a definition because at the highest level of its activity the conscious process is in a continual flux. The link that binds body and mind together is metaphysical in nature and operates through a dialectical escape-relief-creation pattern to produce a mind pitch at every evolutionary stage of life—every cell is an experience complex of escapes-reliefs-creations.

The mind principle of plant life is general in nature and largely confined to the cell itself, since most of the functioning of a plant is controlled from outside sources, such as the sun in photosynthesis and the ground or gravity in osmosis, and there is little need for a complex nervous system. Plants have cellulose walls for a body structure, produce their food by photosynthesis in their leaves and have no true digestive system. (The latter characteristic does not always hold true, for there is a species of alga which not only produces its own food but also has a mouth and a digestive system for living off other organisms.) Plants display less prehensile activity than do animals and show varying degrees of sensitivity, the basis for stimulation and response. Perhaps the main characteristic that separates plant from animal life is the existence of a blind or conscious phase in the latter; animals not only war with the world that is outside of themselves but with the world that is within, and the two must be reconciled by means of a complex nervous system which consists of the instinctive and the intellectual stages. Somehow, animals are able to initiate, or promote, or sustain, an emotional phase that is fairly well balanced at the instinctive level; but if its normal routine is disturbed it is forced to surge to a higher level for correction. In the evolution of the subjective phase there is a long history of development, beginning with a one-cell animal that has only one nerve fibre, one end of which it uses to receive the stimulus and the other to make the response. From this an emotional phase has developed until it constitutes a very complex system. The cycles and rhythms which control the functioning of the internal organs such as the heart and the lungs are impulses which are emotional in nature but have become fixed to a remarkable degree of accuracy during the course of their evolution. In such instances the freedom of the will has become enslaved by the specialization of an emotional phase, much as the physical stage by adaptation. The instinctive-emotional stability of some lower orders of life is almost self-sufficient since they can apparently function normally even after the brain or cephalic ganglion has been severed from the rest of the nervous system; but it exists as tell-tale evidence of a higher correction center. As a rule, however, where freedom avenues are available, the emotional phase has continued to develop; the higher the order or species, the greater is its emotional development, and the lower the order or species, the more specialized is its emotional development, for the will must continue to search for higher physical and emotional development and concentrates its effort where the challenge is the greatest and there is room to enlarge the phase.

In addition to the important role the emotions play in the development of a species as a whole, the emotional phase lends itself readily to emphasis on the individual, and as a general rule the emotional characteristics of the individual and the race develop together. It was Darwin who pointed out that the struggle between the individual members of the same species was often more intense than among the species themselves. This became a large factor in the survival of the species since the strongest males were able to choose the more desirable females and consequently their offspring were better able to survive.

In course of time the mammals developed a more highly organized brain whereby the will was able to differentiate the emotions into finer feelings, which resulted in a more mobile and modifiable life process. Some mammals below man have well-developed emotions; the parental feelings (or instincts, according to their development) have been a large factor in the survival of many species by providing a more enduring attachment between parent and offspring. There can be but little doubt that the emotions are well developed in the higher primates. This is indicated by the almost human range of emotions expressed on their faces; for that reason the anthropoids are placed next to man in the development of the emotions. It is said that the small gibbon displays "a quality of soul" much like that of man in its family relationship; but we must dismiss the belief that there exists a soul in animals below man since the self must be able to idealize in order to have a soul; animals below man have not attained that degree of intellectual freedom.

Darwin concerned himself to a considerable extent with the instincts and emotions of animals, but he regarded all behavior as having physical adaptation as its ultimate aim. He was supported in this view by other naturalists who claimed that certain facial muscles developed solely for the expression of the emotions. We have already pointed out that all stages of life must be physically based, for mass is just as important in preventing the sudden completion of the life process as it is of the universe. But to insist that a physical adaptation is the sole aim of life leads only to confusion when we take into consideration the freer movements of the instinctive and intellectual stages. Therefore, while agreeing with the Darwinians that all life behavior must have a physical base, we shall still hold to our contention that all stages of life are metaphysical in their nature and that the instinctive and the intellectual stages are seeking an ideal balance despite the fact that the ultimate aim of life would be a hypothetical or spiritual whole of completion.

The persistence in the development of the mind principle has been noted long after some species has reached the maximum possibility of its physical development. This is true in certain species of existing rodents when their brain capacity is compared to the fossiled skulls of their tertiary ancestors, and it has been found that the brain capacity of the present day species is much larger than the brain capacity of its ancient progenitors. This is but one of many facts which help to support the theory that there exists an underlying pattern that works towards developing the brain although the physical possibilities have long become exhausted. As an organism of refinement, the life pattern has produced a wide variety of species with many instinctive-emotional and intellectual-feeling balances; for it became increasingly important that the movement attain a higher degree of mobility in order to meet the diverse challenges to existence and so that the emotional disturbances could be stabilized and the feeling phase differentiated by a higher process of reasoning. It would have been impossible for so finely balanced an organism as life to have survived the destruction of the universe if it had not achieved a measure of dominance over it by its rationality.

The theory that life can be explained as a constructive embodiment of phases and stages of lessening tension leads logically to the conclusion that both instinctive behavior and intellectual experience can be explained as the activity of a metaphysical phase; intellectual experience and instinctive behavior are not inherited; instead, certain physical conditions or biological aptitudes are inherited which are transformed into a behavior or experience complex by stimulation and response. Through the use of a dialectical escape-relief-creation pattern that compels the phase to seek a better balance, the instincts may be regarded as congenital modes or balances of behavior which contribute to the experience complex when disturbed and cause the conscious process to make an adjustment that, in turns, corrects or modifies the instinctive behavior or perhaps may eventually modify the physical adaptation. Darwin wrote that his theory of evolution would "cause a whole of metaphysics"; it is the pitch of the discordant emotions from the instinctive to the intellectual stage which causes the will to seek an ultimate whole of metaphysics—the conscious impression of reality.

CHAPTER XIII

The Phase, the Stage, the Phase

DURING THE COURSE of a long evolution the sensory organs became well diversified and specialized, for it was necessary that the will receive a variety of sense impressions and co-ordinate them through a common center so as to transmit their messages to many parts of the body; the unification of many centers produced very complex centers, such as the cerebellum and the cerebrum. The development of the brain is dependent upon the specific task with which it is confronted. The cerebellum of the bird is well developed for it is necessary that this division of its brain attain a high degree of sophistication in order to control the wing muscles in flying. The dinosaur was able to function with a brain that was quite small considering its huge size—a high intellectual development was not of prime importance for its survival. The rodent, however, which replaced the giant lizard as the dominant land animal, had a large brain rela-tive to its small body size and, with the advent of the mam-mal intelligence, the cerebrum took on an increasing impor-tance. In man, the cerebrum is so well developed that it has become convoluted and spills over all the other divisions of the brain, which indicates the large amount of both raw and organized experience tissue that is needed in the processes of reasoning.

The difference between the intelligence of man and that of the lower animals was believed by Darwin to be one of degree and not of kind, and he considered man to be the animal which has the smallest number of instincts. Professor William James, on the other hand, thought man to be the animal with the greatest number of instincts. The difference in their opinion is best compromised by stating that man is the animal with the largest number of instincts that are modifiable. All experience is dependent upon racial preparation and is more or less modifiable. Perceptual experience is almost entirely dependent upon racial preparation and is shared by both man and animals alike in its varying degree of development. Conceptual experience is dependent upon individual preparation and is shared only by man and possibly a few higher animals. The progress of man is correlated to his ability to be educated, and that is dependent upon the primary experience tissue which has been modified through racial development or on pliable brain tissue which can be modified by man himself. Australopithecus —the half-man and half-ape of a million years ago—did not remain a hairy brute, because there was always a sufficient amount of brain tissue which could be modified.

Life, in order to escape destruction, has been forced into a higher and more refined stage of development because it was necessary that the will seek a complete relief. The intensification of the effort becomes so great at the intellectual stage that the will leaps over the lower stages with plans or ideas of a more complete reality. Each test begins with the urging of the will and ends with the best possible adjustment. The realm of ideas is the field of play and gladiatorial arena where all mortal mental combats take place through conscious efforts to relieve the tensions of life. A constant challenge motivates a psychic phenomenon by which a continual experience pattern is created in a conscious being. Awareness is the end result of the development of raw sensations that have arisen out of the sensory organs and consist of the development of stimuli and responses. Sensations which arise within and without the organism may be recognized as discordant at the instinctive level and passed on to the conscious processes, to be corrected by an idea until the emotional disturbance is relieved. Thus, the phrase "emotional disturbance" may be regarded as a phase relationship between the higher and somewhat less stabilized stage of the intellect and the lower and usually more stablized stage of the instincts. The adjustment which takes place between the poles of the movement comprises the processes of reasoning of a conscious phase. At the intellectual stage, the stabilization process plays between the stable and unstable factors of ideas. The escape takes place through awareness; the relief is in a plan or idea to relieve the tension; and the creation is a freedom concept or a distinguishable feeling. Through ideas, the objective states of existence—that which is aimed at—are brought into agreement or harmony with the subjective phase of being— that which is—and there is a reconciliation between the instinctive and the intellectual stages as the conscious phase continues to release itself through the process of negation. Between the poles of pleasure and pain all emotional activity takes place. Metaphysically, all sensitivity contains the factors of stability and instability, a primordial plus and minus; every stimulation is followed by a response which has its correlative in the reality process. Schopenhauer reminds us: Pain is positive, pleasure is negative—the pleasurable feelings fade away as they are released from their restrictions.

Ideas as plans to relieve the tensions of life are in constant demand throughout the thinking process, and the will, by the imperative of refinement, must always have available sufficient plans from which to choose. At the intellectual stage the will is conscious of its ideas as it tries to choose the concordant plans over the discordant ones. If it is successful, it will cause a lessening of sensorial pressure. Whenever a plan to relieve a tension is successful, it is stored in the durable tissues of the brain as a freedom concept so that it can be used again for future reference. And as ideas are systematically posited in the experience complex, the brain itself becomes more stabilized. However, if the emotional disturbance is not at first relieved, it must be returned to again and again until the tension is relieved by another idea. Somehow, the conscious phase is able to dip into the previous store of ideas which offer a variety of plans. Through the diversity of biological pressures, variety in unity has become the law of the intellect, but due to the numerous plans from which to choose, the intellectual stage is more experimental than are the lower stages, and the chance of error is much greater.

The emotional disturbances which arise out of the instinctive stage remind us of the combination of different colors in a light ray. Just as the emotions are composed of many sensations, there is likewise no true color in an ordinary light ray since it consists of many different colors. The desired color must first be absorbed by a special gaseous filament and amplified by an electronic device called a laser before a pure light beam can be emitted at its aperture. At the intellectual stage a somewhat analogous result is accomplished: the conscious process of reasoning differentiates and specializes the emotions into a variety of feelings. Identity occurs here by means of the phase, the stage, the phase. There is no intellectual activity without a distinguishable feeling. John Dewey said, "Feeling is the activity of the self and the self is as wide as the range of experience. Although feeling refers to an object, it belongs to the self." The self always tries to realize itself through the impression of wholeness and it directs all activity towards that end. When feeling reaches the highest degree of categorization, it leaves the fullest impression of reality.

The intellectual stage represents the highest metaphysical accomplishment of life and completes the effort of the will through the category of refinement to achieve a full balance of harmony by the use of an emotional phase; the upshot is a continuous phase—the self or soul. At the final metaphysical stage of life a conscious entity is suspended through the negation of feeling as it reaches out to grasp an ultimate reality and tries to complete itself by means of its idealizations. Here, too, the self is able to hop a free ride in a world of fancy as it soars over a wave of pleasurable feelings, probably following the advice of the poet Keats:

> *Ever let the Fancy roam,*
> *Pleasure never is at home.*

We can no more stop a feeling and examine its parts than we can stop the physical processes and examine their energy. Feeling is unleashed biological freedom. Any attempt to explain the higher releases of life solely in terms of physical adaptation is as impossible as was that of the physicist of the past century to explain the physical world solely as matter. As a metaphysical stream, consciousness is always in the process of becoming; it is never a noumenon or thing-in-itself. At the highest and most refined phase of its activity it creates the finest feelings as a categorical necessity of the will for survival, as the self or soul, which constitutes the embodiment of the stream, searches for the fullest completion. Value has now become not just another physical adaptation or an instinctive-emotional balance, but the net worth of the finer feelings which are being weighed on the intellectual scales of being, and it comprises an ever-transcending soul of harmony. The psychologist is quite correct when he states that feelings have content since they comprise balanced wholes of harmony. Aesthetic, intellectual and religious feelings afford the soul its finest values, the most complete release from the discordance of existence. And they become the highest spiritual directive towards a hypothetical balance of harmony which the soul symbolizes as God; the more perfectly developed the soul of man, the more resplendent is his God as he idealizes and endeavors to complete himself in an ideal or spiritual realm. Such a hypothetical goal of harmonies by means of a suspended life entity like the soul would compose a realm of pure spirituality, and if such a state was possible of attainment it would become the fourth metaphysical stage of life. It is a goal, however, which can only be attained by the continual expenditure of physical and emotional energy, which is primarily dependent upon the energy of the sun which is a part of the irrational universe as it impels the soul in its process of idealization. At the highest point of intellectual intensification the soul is analogous to the rays of the dying sun as it expends its energy and gradually grows colder; but whereas the sun gradually grows dimmer, the soul of man becomes brighter and enhances in value as it

81

pursues its eternal search for a finer balance of harmony. This is what is meant by a constructive life-process as opposed to a destructive universal one; but both movements must use the same escape-relief-creation pattern to create their realities.

As the conscious stream has developed out of the blindness of the lower stages of life, it has developed a self which is chained forever to the appeasement of an irrational universe; and as man has learned to idealize, he has developed the self into a soul. The irony of the soul is that it is a phase and must complete itself by means of its idealizations. In a moment of ecstasy the voyager might fancy that his soul has taken flight as it sets forth on an imaginary journey, riding very swiftly over a wave of pleasurable feelings that keep negating themselves into nothingness. As a sojourner in such an imaginary state, the soul is free to direct the course of its destiny—far from the strife of a mundane world—as it searches for an ideal haven of harmony. But in the new world of freedom the voyager has become a mystic and a dreamer, where fancy plays the dominant role. However, if the imagination is permitted to develop freely, the soul will continue its search for a spiritual whole of completion. It might be well to regard the imagination as in the process of developing the eyes of the soul; whereas nature has endowed man with sight to distinguish colors, the imagination has not yet completed all the mystical hues for the soul. By means of the imagination, a rational life pattern is converted into a God-pattern, as in Judeo-Christian-Islamic religions, or a negation pattern, as in the Buddhist religion. In the latter case it is utterly inconsistent with the metaphysical aim of life.

The feeling for the mystical is a part of the soul's longing for completion. It is possible that a "mystical conception" or a "divine intuition" was written into the subconscious mind of a religious devotee by a practical escape-relief-creation pattern long before we ever embarked on our flight to eternity and was used as a means of explaining the relationship between life and the universe. Most often, however, the world of the mystic is a dream world in which an ideal whole has become fancifully balanced, but where it occasionally bumps into a practical world of reality and is forced to make an adjustment to it. Rather than forgo a world of pleasant dreams, the mystic withdraws from the practical world and seeks his peace of mind in seclusion.

Since it has been the contention of our voyage that all that is, is real, it would follow as a corollary that dreams are real too. Dreams are momentarily real, but not necessarily true; truth is based upon a more solid whole of relationship. In the case of the mystic, a dream has become the haven of a blind religious soul that is seeking a balance by means of the finer feelings and is somewhat analogous to the blind will of the instinctive stage that is seeking a balance by means of an emotional phase. In the case of the mystic, the balance is sought at the highest metaphysical stage of life based upon the faith and hope of an erring being. Whenever such a mystical state exists, the religious devotee has fallen victim to a false intellectual pursuit.

There can be little doubt that true religiosity is a part of the higher metaphysical releases of life and that imagination does have a definite survival value and probably will have an even greater value as man seeks means of employing his leisure time in an age of automation. We are at the beginning of an age of thought which will most likely be dominated by some form of materialistic humanism for the next one thousand years; but whatever increments might be gained by the new system of thinking, man will still be poor if he is not able to enlarge upon his conceptual values by means of his imagination. Man is an exceptional animal, not merely because he is able to communicate and perpetuate his thought to others but also because of the superiority of his imagination.

CHAPTER XIV

Summary to Part Two

THREE METAPHYSICAL stages of life have been explored on the present part of our journey: the physical stage is basic to life in order to prevent its sudden completion; the instinctive and the intellectual stages promote and refine an emotional phase which is the clue to the ultimate though hypothetical goal that life is seeking by means of a dialectical realism. Many orders and species do not contain all three stages since there was not sufficient room available for their development; but each higher stage contains the one or more stages that preceded its development—as life is seeking a solution to its destiny by increasing its mobility. The phase always precedes the stage in the development of life; this is opposite to the process of the universe, where the stage always precedes the phase. Without this important distinction the goals of the two movements cannot be determined. Both movements, however, are metaphysical in nature, and each is working through the same practical escape-relief-creation pattern to resolve the difference between their stable and unstable factors and to achieve a final balance. The intermediate balances represent their fleeting realities, and since the goal of life is different from that of the universe it is inconsistent with that movement.

Life as a reality-process is difficult to define. The movement consists of the evolution of constructive phases and stages that must perpetually be posited against the destructive stages and phases of the universe as the will becomes better organized as an instrument of refinement. This constitutes the natural law of refinement through the category of refinement and is a built-in process of reasoning at every metaphysical stage of life. By it, the will is able to meet every challenge to its existence with a more complete whole of reality. As the tensions of life decrease by the increase of its harmonies, it keeps positing them against the decreasing reality-wholes of the universe throughout a complexity of stages and phases by phases and stages—a pluralistic manifestation with a monistic goal of balanced harmonies. Life, however, has never found a complete adjustment in any of its phases and stages, so an irrational universe keeps carrying it along with it on its destructive flight to eternity. The end of the universe will come some day in an all absorbing negation—a patternless stream of motion. But if life is to be partially successful it must always remain constructive and complete its movement as far as possible within the framework of the universe which will end with the dissolution of that reality.

The will would never have tried so hard to adapt itself to such a hostile environment, nor would it have created such wealth in variety and numbers through its divisions, differentiations and specializations, nor would it have passed the increments on to untold generations, if it had not had from the beginning an ultimate aim of completion inherent in its governing pattern. Although the course of life has often been stagnant and uncertain, the overall goal of balanced harmonies is manifested throughout the stages of evolution as higher and more complex forms of life are created, where each developing phase and stage consists of an orchestration of cycles and rhythms in a continually mounting crescendo until the soul of man has emerged, which is conscious of its striving for an ideal goal, which the self symbolizes as a perfect idea and the soul as God. The more finely developed the self or soul, the more perfect is the idea and the more resplendent is the God as man endeavors to complete himself ideally or spiritually.

Man has a longer period of intellectual development when compared to his physical development. The end of his physical development is usually reached in his early twenties; soon afterwards there begins a slow decline which continues until his death. Man's full intellectual development, however, is often not reached until he gains the age of thirty, and even then it retains an option of further development. Some of the apparent development is undoubtedly due to the large amount of experience which is acquired after man reaches thirty, which enables him to make much better decisions. But most of the latter development is due to the greater plasticity of the brain tissues which enables them to be moulded into an experience complex at a later period of life. It seems, too, that the brain tissues have a greater durability than do those of the body, and this has been confirmed by experiments in the laboratory where it has been found that the tissues of the body are replaced several times during the course of a lifetime whereas the brain tissues are rarely replaced and some, perhaps, are never replaced. This fact might help to explain how objects are recalled from memory over the entire lifetime of an individual.

There are many factors that contribute to natural death, but the primary one is that each of the three metaphysical stages of life maintains the greatest balance possible during the span of an individual life cycle. It exhausts the possibility of further development and maintenance and dies. The destructive material encasement of the universal reality gradually closes in on the more delicately balanced harmonies of life and attains the inevitable mastery; the tissues harden, the muscles become less resilient, the bones calcify, and there is a general waning in the functioning of the body.

An effort has been made in Part I and Part II to answer the question as to where the world is going and why, but we have yet to fully answer the question as to whether it has a reasonable prospect of getting there. In Part III, the concluding part of our journey, we shall be concerned with the implementation of the self or soul by means of freedom concepts as the life process continues to release itself from the irrationalism of the universe and the blind rationalization of the will, opening the doors wider for a fuller metaphysical completion.

Part III

THE RELEASE FROM BLINDNESS

CHAPTER XV

Preface to Part Three

DURING OUR VOYAGE we have endeavored to establish the relationship between the movement of the universe and the movement of life by showing how both the regression of the universe and the progression of life are a part of the reality which is in all things. It is displayed by the universe in an irrational way and developed by life in three metaphysical stages: both movements become freer as they release themselves from tension; at the more fluid and mobile stage of life the releases become the highest conceptual values of a sentimental man as he strives to complete himself by means of his idealizations. Due to the intimate relationship between life and the universe, life is more than a movement to be completed in the immediate present, for as life releases itself in evolutionary stages from restrictions it develops a constant stream of finer balances, weaves them into higher cycles and rhythms, and passes them on to the next generation in a greater symphony of value. It was the expectation of permanently escaping from the destructive universe that laid the foundation for the faith of rational man as he gradually developed himself into a soul and endeavored to complete himself in an ideal or spiritual realm.

There is little basis for faith or hope if we stop to examine the early beginning of life. We might look in vain for the ideal in the torrid seas or humid air where life had its first beginning and where the first pattern was to become the pattern for all life forms to follow, down the stretch of two billion years. There is evidence to support the theory that life existed in a boneless form for more than three times as long as its fossilized history. Its rationality was not only blind but very general in nature, and the species consisted mostly of insentient creatures that were more interested in division than in differentiation. But the will was so tireless in achieving a balance of harmony that it eventually filled the sea and land with serpents and monsters; and after some back-filling it ushered in the Age of Mammals and then, finally, man. Despite its wastefulness, the will built a world of reality as an imperative of refinement, for it was compelled to do so to find relief, and relief is only found in the finer patterns. All the beauty in nature, all that is good in life, all that compels the will to seek something higher, is the result of the omnipotent pressure for refinement. Inevitably, the intensification of the effort led to the development of the finer feelings which are the conscious values of life. At the intellectual stage the category of refinement becomes the category of finer feelings and is the most modifiable and freest metaphysical movement of life, as fresh opportunities are opened to relieve the tensions of life by means of conscious laws. Because it has been necessary for man to continue his metaphysical development, the finer feelings, being the highest releases of life through freedom concepts, have provided the basis for the institutions of the free world—the arts, the sciences and the religions—which help impart a stability to life as an ideal or spiritual whole of completion. We shall be concerned on the last lap of our journey with these ideal and spiritual balances, the reality of which is so much like that of the universe but so different in aim and fulfillment.

CHAPTER XVI

The Practical and the Ideal

SINCE the intellectual stage developed as a necessity of refinement, it followed the biological urge to achieve unity through variety and subsequently developed a pattern of knowledge, a pattern of faith, and a pattern of form; all three are facets of the same escape-relief-creation pattern. Through the differentiation of the inverted pattern, life became the basis for a more complex evolutionary development, by means of which the gulf that separates the aim of life and its fulfillment was narrowed and an outline of the ideal or spiritual goal could be formulated. Sentimental man, as he idealizes, is engaged in a romantic search of it. The possibilities are as great as when the universe began its long flight out of a primal tension center and pluralistically sought an ultimate cessation from all tension by an absorption in a sea of negation. The goal of life, so conceived, is constructive and comprehensive: as it tries to embrace a greater whole of reality by means of the higher conceptual feelings as they release the self from the blindness of the past.

There are two aspects to the fulfillment of life, namely, the practical and the ideal. The practical goes to appease an irrational universe and is forced upon the life movement by the inexorable and relentless physical processes of the universe. The ideal belongs to the self or soul of harmony, or God, which is rational. The conflict that ensues when the practical balances that must appease an irrational universe vie with the ideal wholes which are striving to achieve a completion in a hypothetical realm consists of a dualism in the many and various ways in which life is endeavoring to complete itself.

Due to the greater flexibility of the intellect when compared with the lower metaphysical stages of life, the most successful effort to transform the ideal into the practical and the practical into the ideal is through the conscious process of reasoning. Here, as an experimental phase, the self or soul can search for an ideal completion by means of the practical balances, or a practical balance by means of an ideal projection, for at the more fluid stage of the intellect the life pattern can reason from the particular to the general and from the general to the particular since the reasoning process is reversible and each is a part of the self's search for completion.

At the intellectual stage, as at the lower metaphysical stages, the will is seeking a completion by means of a practical pattern and both the ideal and the practical comprise its mode of operation; each is a fundamental part of life's long evolutionary development whereby it tries to release itself from the restrictions of the physical world and the blindness of the lower stages, and searches eternally for new avenues of freedom. Man's constantly expanding horizons consist of a growing faith in the perfection and completion of his culture and his civilization, and there has been an increased acceleration in the effort as he has learned to enlarge his conceptual wholes. As man has learned through freedom concepts to rationalize, the category of form has become the arts, the category of knowledge has become the specialized sciences, and the category of faith has become the mystical wholes of organized religion. The pressure for a practical as well as an ideal completion has become so persistent that there is an increasing demand for a fuller realization, and the impulsion is creating new breakthroughs in all the fields of art, science and religion. And the more practical idealists are seeking further means of implementing the progress of mankind through less restricted ideas.

Many of the ideals of man have achieved a measure of practicability within the limited confines of their framework; none, however, represent final wholes of completion in themselves. This is because, should all the religious, aesthetic and scientific aims of life become fully realizable they would cease to be the ideal wholes of reality—they would become its practical wholes. However, there have been several noteworthy attempts in past history to accomplish this. By means of their aesthetic realism, the Greeks achieved a remarkable utility of aim; it became the basis for their culture and was later to provide the foundation for many of the cultures of the West. The ecclesiastical realism of the Middle Ages tried to merge the ideal wholes of art, science and religion by means of a rigid Church dogma. But the world of the Churchmen was a fantasy world of saints and angels that a new scientific realism was soon to awaken to a modern world of a physical reality, which, in turn, was largely destroyed by science itself during the present century when it was demonstrated that mass was equivalent to energy.

An expanding idealism has prompted man to create new freedom concepts and he has devised various institutions to assist in fulfilling his aims. The three realistic movements previously mentioned were the result of man's desire for a greater freedom of expression by the enlargement of the conceptual wholes of reality; but all three movements were basically idealistic movements, for in each the enlargement of the idealizations of man produced a continually widening field of scientific, religious and artistic expression of his infinite possibility. The stream of political idealism which had its beginning with the Greeks found democratic procedure a means of implementing the goal of a perfect society, and it is continuing today as new means of communication and transportation make the political world grow smaller and necessitate a common bond to help eradicate the suffering and misery of the masses and prevent a disastrous war in the future. While the social and the political ideals of man have yet to bear ripened fruit, the goals of a perfect society are perhaps more realizable today than at any other period in the history of mankind.

CHAPTER XVII

The Release from Blindness

WHERE THE WILL became better organized in its rationality it was more successful and was able to mould its experience into rules of behavior which gave a surer direction to its striving for stability. But the next step had to always lie practically ahead as it reached ideally towards a hypothetical balance of harmony. We have already found the development towards a hypothetical balance of harmony manifested, even at the lowest metaphysical stage of life, through the creation of organic unity; at the instinctive stage it is found in emotional stability, such as the rhythmical reoccurrence of impulse cycles; and at the intellectual stage it has become a conscious impulsion through the development of freedom concepts which furnish the basis for the idealizations of man. Ideals are not an illusion, because they are based upon the more imaginative conceptual experience—because at the higher mobile phase of conscious reasoning, the harmonies of life are developing towards a greater freedom in a growing whole of spirituality that no longer recognizes a limit to life's striving.

The progress of man towards a greater freedom is dependent upon his ability to conceive a larger whole of reality; the mind develops towards a more complete conception of reality whenever it reacts to the conditions that challenge its survival, and if it cannot, it succumbs to another mind which has the flexibility. The laws of conscious reasoning are no more than escape-relief-creation patterns which work as a category of refinement and which govern all biological processes towards a greater whole of completion. As they enlarge the freedom of life and as they accomplish their purpose, they increase the rationality of life over the irrationality of the universe. Intellectual freedom, for the savage, is the same escape from restrictions as it is for the civilized man, as the will strives for an ever increasingly greater release from the blindness of its past. Wonder has furnished the inspiration for the human mind to erect a superstructure of ideals in order to accommodate the expanding harmonies which the will persists in creating; as it does so it moulds its experience pattern into a developing higher phase and stage of wholeness and reflects a life of growing freedom.

Man is tied to his past conceptions of freedom, which are partly false and partly true due to the insufficiency of their development. He is never more than half free, but the extent of the freedom he has achieved has led to the desire for a greater freedom. He realizes he has a vast span to cover before he can achieve a final balance or complete whole. He projects an ideal and tries to balance it against the measurable side of his being, which is an evolutionary development through the category of refinement. By an ideal projection, a metaphysical phase hopes to find a final haven where there is no strife and where there is a perfect adjustment with the universe of action. By such an ideal projection the dread of reality is broken and a chain is forged from the past to the present and into the future as the will continues in its impulse for a perfect balance.

Rousseau in his early sentimentalism expressed the belief that it is the natural qualities of man which are the finest and the most enduring; later, as he grew older, he argued that civilization has defiled the natural simplicity of man and that man's only hope is to return to the primitivism of his past. It is true that life is seeking an emotional-feeling stability at the intellectual level and that, also, there are primitive people living today who have achieved a high degree of emotional-feeling stability due to their long terrestrial adaptation where the tenor of life is from day to day and there is little cause to worry about tomorrow. However, there are civilized races living today that have been

forced to undergo a large amount of emotional-feeling instability due to the lack of a terrestrial adaptation. As a
result they have been forced to think beyond today and
worry about a tomorrow, and consequently have developed
a higher conception of freedom. The salvation of man is
not to return to the primitive limitations of his past but to
continue his triumph over irrationalism. Rousseau, by his
philosophy, would turn the mind of man backward. But
the freely activated mind of a civilized man, while recog-
nizing the natural stream which underlies life, would aug-
ment it with a freer stream of idealism and thereby acceler-
ate man's progress towards an ideal or spiritual balance
through the finer conceptual feelings.

Schopenhauer regarded the denial of the will as the
only escape from the misery of the world, but the free mind
reasons that the harmonies of life open up fresh opportunities to further alleviate the discordance of existence as
they integrate into larger wholes of lessening tension by
means of freedom concepts. Since the free mind is able to
escape from its bondage, antithesis and discordance are only
obstacles to overcome as life searches for a more permanent balance. The aspiration for a perfect life is one of
man's most cherished dreams, and he has created the highest conceptual releases to remove him as far as possible
from the discordance of existence. To have survived as an
organism of refinement, life has been under a constant
pressure. A restlessness has been imparted by an irrational
universe and a blind will to a child of ideas who is seeking
an ideal or spiritual realm by means of the freshest streams
of freedom that affords the widest latitude in man's effort
to achieve a complete balance. A sentimental man as a partially free agent, in trying to escape the tensions of life,
has developed the finer concepts because they give the surest
direction in his effort to achieve that end.

Blind rationalization as a mere factor of adaptation
would never have developed the finer feelings; nor would
there have ever evolved the mind of a partially free man
who is trying to conceive or embrace the whole of life and
the universe as he assumes control of his physical and spir-

96

itual destiny. But man is attempting to do this with the development of his conceptual feelings. With the growing realization of the place of freedom in the scheme of both life and the universe, man does not intend to relinquish the right to control his ultimate destiny to a philosophy of primitivism—which would mean his enslavement to the false ideologies of the past. While the desire for freedom is greater in some than in others, mankind has been fortunate that it has been able to produce individual men of lofty leadership with a higher conception of freedom who have been able to instill the desire for a greater freedom in their fellow men. It may be recalled that even at the lower metaphysical stages of life, wherever the door of freedom has been left open, the attainment of a higher ideal balance has been successful.

Whereas in the past the primitive mind conceived the goal by ignorance and superstition, it is today being perceived through knowledge which is based upon fact. The mind of civilized man has not yet created all the freedom concepts that will fully express the image whole and release mankind from the blind rationalization which clings like a tight garment around all forms of life; because man is a part of a long biological development of lessening tension, the freedom concepts are difficult to formulate. It is the tendency of most lower animals to exhaust the possibility of their evolutionary development and sink into a dream-like state or coma by means of an instinctive-emotional balance. Even the freer mind of man is susceptible to blind balances and, like the lower species, relapses into a dream state or mystical balance which affords the largest emotional pleasure with the least amount of mental disturbance until there is little freedom left at the intellectual stage. Here a phase is in the process of establishing a biological law of resistance to change.

For an ideal to be of any practical benefit it must be possible of fulfillment—a place where the ideal and the real can meet. It was never the aim of life merely to increase the adaptation alone but to refine harmonies until they become a balance of rationality. While the harmonies of the lower species are standards of value within the restricted world of a particular species, adaptive values are not the surest guide for the intellectual stage of man, for such a goal of balanced harmonies requires the highest freedom concepts. Biologically it is a development, metaphysically it is a release. As an evolutionary concept which is ideally and spiritually symbolic we shall introduce a new phrase and call it activated sentimentalism. Sentimentalism is the doctrine of finer feelings, and activated means that which is consciously impelled towards an ideal or spiritual completion by a practical escape-relief-creation pattern. Being the evolutionary concept of the finer feelings, it is not the apotheosis of feeling over reason, because reason is built into every metaphysical stage by the inverted life process through the category of refinement. It is a rational doctrine of a partially free man in a dynamic and changing world whose aspirations must be nourished with the minimum of restrictions.

A moral base is essential to the activation of the finer feeling and helps to guide the self beyond the brutality, sensuality and avariciousness of smaller and more restricted moral wholes as it direct the metaphysical phase towards higher releases. Sympathy arises from the universalization of the moral feelings and the magnanimous soul seeks the companionship of other souls in a growing whole of humanity. Sympathy, devotion and courage universalize themselves in a constantly widening field of social, political and religious development and become the basis for a more finely organized structure which is created by love and brotherhood. It is for this reason that the moral feelings are the most mature of the finer feelings since they are the creation of the soul with other souls in a growing whole of humanity, by which the increment is returned to the individual as a stabilizing factor which he shares with the rest of humanity. While moral feelings are the most mature of the finer feelings, they may become restricted by rigid moral codes. Often a master morality of one period in history is regarded as a slave morality by the next.

A man is often judged by the steadfastness that accrues

from his moral strivings. Yet, the moral man is the free man; freedom and virtue, morality and intelligence are closely related in the development of the soul and are a part of the foundation of man's being as he seeks the reality of truth, beauty and goodness. Institutions which permit the largest amount of freedom are the ones most likely to set the highest moral standards and produce the largest number of virtuous people. Much of the freedom, however, that man has wrested from the blindness and repressive conditions of the past has in many instances been achieved by trial and error and has brought him only a little less enslavement and a somewhat imperfect conception as to what is the ideal morality. But despite the difficulties that besets Man's effort to lift himself to a higher plane of being, he has somehow been able, where conditions have been favorable to the fulfillment of life as an idealistic adventure, to promote institutions that foster the freer conceptual releases of truth, beauty and goodness; and they have become a part of his developing reality, and his eternal search for completion.

CHAPTER XVIII

Cultures and Civilizations

PRIMITIVE MAN became a new frontiersman quite early in his history, for he was destined to journey to faraway places where he had to adjust himself to new surroundings. In our fancy we might imagine when he came to some spot in the wilderness and chose it for his home: he paused momentarily in wonderment, because the challenges it presented could have not been less than mentally stimulating—in the untamed wilderness there was the fascination of that which is different, a newfound freedom and a virgin soil that had never been touched by another man's hand, where a new start in life could begin that was far removed from the restriction of the old home which had been left behind. It is noteworthy that man, in his progress towards a larger freedom, began from the start to ask the meaning of things, and as he did he found ways of implementing his progress. He not only learned new things but made good use of his knowledge. And the development of the hands so closely parallels the development of the mind that it is sometimes difficult to say whether it has been the hands which have educated the mind, or whether it has been the mind that has educated the hands. Should there be any question in the voyager's mind he is only to remember that the inverted life pattern had something else in view other than a physical adaptation. By continually developing his skill man has progressed from the crude stick plow of antiquity to the modern tractor, from numbers laboriously carved on stone to the modern computer. As man has enlarged the practical wholes of land and animal husbandry he has also enlarged his social, political and economic structure. Historians note that a civilization has usually followed the introduction of wheat into a barbarian land; with it has come the other refinements that change an ancient way of life into a modern one.

The progress of man towards a greater freedom is manifested in the arts and sciences, which increase his leisure and also lead him to appreciate the finer things in life. The discovery of fire began a long history of scientific, artistic and cultural progress that was eventually to change man's entire clothing, sheltering and eating habits. Fire is so basic to the cultures of mankind that it is even reflected in the races of today; the Caucasian and Mongolian races have an unbroken record in the use of fire, dating back to its discovery by primitive man, and are far more advanced culture-wise than are the Australoid and Negroid races, where its use was broken for a considerable period of time before being resumed.

There is a maturation of a people which accompanies their refinement and which provides a basis for the further accumulation of their culture. We may regard a society as an organization of people who have grown to maturity through the increased wholes or aspects of refinement, and a civilization as an accumulation of cultures. As civilizations have developed out of the cultures of the past, they have provided a greater stability to the politico-social-economic organizations for which they exist. The nature of the organizations is such, however, that it becomes necessary for them to constantly strive to alleviate the conflict which rises within. As they are successful they grow progressively less pliable; all human organizations are likely to grow more rigid. Subsequently they must inevitably give way to a new civilization which holds a greater promise for the future. The mingling of new blood with old brings an additional stimulus by inculcating the refinements of the older culture with the freshness of a more primitive one. As a result a new escape-relief-creation pattern is formed.

A state as a unit or the unit of a civilization is an organization governed by a practical escape-relief-creation pattern which is working as a category of refinement as it tries to right the balances of nations. The state has many complex factors in its political, social and economic structure, and it is these that are the most contested. Sooner or later all governments are forced into a period of adjustment, or else they collapse under the constant pressure for a complete adjustment. The escape takes place, the relief is found and a new creation arises that becomes the basis for a better social, political and economic organization. As a rule this is the normal course of human events and in the long run makes for a healthier condition of some future society if it is conducive to the growth and fulfillment of its practical and ideal aims.

A classic example of the integration of the stable and unstable factors of a primitive and culturally advanced people can be found in the conquest of the old Greeks by "the fair-haired Titans." The consolidation that followed resulted in "the glory that was Greece," which was to later become the foundation of Western civilization. A good example of a social and political order that attained a high degree of stability so that its people were satisfied with their way of life can be found in old Chinese civilization that began four thousand years ago. But this civilization finally collapsed under a population explosion and the Western civilization that kept knocking at its door; today, there is a new China, one that is in transition from the old way of life to a modern one. But the Chinese have had to change both their political and social structure. Among the progressive nations of the West, the people of the German Empire developed a splendid culture but were unable to grow out of a narrow nationalism which caused two disastrous world wars. After the last war, West Germany formed an alliance with her sister nations that has enabled her to maintain her existing culture and at the same time alleviate her international tension by peaceful means.

Brute force plays a powerful role in the history of man and this is especially true in war. But as man has advanced from the more primitive to the higher cultures we find him becoming more dependent upon the finer things of life to sustain the advantages he has gained. Modern refinements have come down from the older cultures which have been passed from one generation to another and have gradually accumulated into the arts and sciences of today, and with them has come the dignity and respect of a free man. Each higher stage of an advancing civilization endeavors to correct the maladjustments of the preceding one, and as we approach nearer our own time we can clearly see the result of man's effort to free himself from ignorance and superstition. As man has been more successful in balancing his institutions of freedom, they have become more refined and practical. There has been an increase in the diversity of the arts and the sciences, and from this diversity there have arisen many institutions of learning whereby man is able to climb to a vantage point and survey the prospects for a still greater progress.

CHAPTER XIX

The Pattern of Knowledge

SINCE THE UNIVERSE and all its varying wholes of reality are in a continual adjustment to the stable, the normal and the complete, the same is true of the processes of knowledge. Thought revolves around a complexity of tension stages, whether concrete or universal, practical or idealistic. It has already been stated that knowledge has developed out of a world of physical objects where the balances are long and durable enough that they can be distinguished from one another through the process of reasoning. As balances they consist of the adjustment between the stable and unstable factors of reality as stages and phases or phases and stages of lessening tension. Stabilization is mirrored throughout the processes of life but the pattern that governs all things is persistent in its effort to equalize the movement. It was the urge for stability which initially caused the will to seek a complete relief as it synthesized its experience into objects of wholeness; the identification of the objects with the inner harmony was the approach to reality by categories of knowledge as the will tried to achieve the best possible adjustment in a world of infinite tension.

We might ask: What does the will find in the processes of knowledge to qualify the stable and the normal of the objective world of reality throughout its complexity of stages? It is its creative effort as the movement releases itself from tension by the development of stabilization stages; in the experience complex, knowledge is the moderator between the rational movement of life and the irrational movement of the universe in an increasing or decreasing whole of displacement. Here all the world becomes a vast transformism of successive stages and phases and phases and stages in an ever increasing balance of reality's stable and unstable factors. The effort of the will to stabilize itself is an extension of the infinitely large and the infinitely small at the various stages of its metaphysical development since the universe and life have yet to realize all of their potential balances and thereby achieve a full completion. The practical and ideal possibilities of the ever-changing balances impart to existence the only unity that is open to it until the processes are completed.

Knowledge is useful in the measurement of the universal and human relationship but it is never complete, and for that reason we cannot conceive space and time with an end or without an end. Categories of knowledge like time and space, motion and rest, etc., are practical approaches to reality and are useful in the present and the immediate future; but where they extend into the unlimited future they have very little meaning for the theorist. It is because knowledge is relative that it has practical value; it is only when we attempt to synthesize objects into ultimately completed reals that it loses its practical value. The development of knowledge equals the measurable whole which has been experienced by racial development or the pliability of the individual and is a development out of the past flight from tension that has found expression by pyramiding experience upon experience. Experience is a never-ending occurrence in life as it refines and balances itself from one constructive stage to that of another; however, it is little more than blind rationalization at the physical and the instinctive stages. Through the pattern of knowledge, language has become the symbol of experience and words the symbol of language where the rationality of life contests the irrationality of the universe as it searches for a solution to its destiny.

Science has progressed from a restricted to a freer rationalization to the degree that truths have been established by practical knowledge. There are many signs that indicate it will continue to do so as new freedoms are provided by an increase of knowledge through new laws and categories which will furnish better means of classification and systematization; for it is unlikely that the older systems of knowledge will be sufficient in an age of abstraction and lightning computers. As man has progressed through the increase of knowledge, he has been able to solve many of nature's mysteries and banish many myths; he has become the master of his destiny largely by the extension of his intellectual pursuits, which are expressed by more complete symbols as he sets the stage for future advancement with the freedom to choose the highest standards for his developing rationalism. Through the constant search for the true, the purposeful and the beautiful, he reaches out to embrace a larger whole of reality until he seems to be a strange mixture of the loftiest ideals and the basest motives of a mind which he carries with him into a new epoch—a world where everything changes except the pattern that governs all reality to a completion.

As man has freed himself by increasing his knowledge, he has opened new avenues through which he is able to build his utopias and heavens with an increasing magnitude and splendor. The projection which he creates forms the basis for his future hopes and symbolizes the yearning of an incompleted man as he endeavors to identify himself with the perfect ideal which embraces a world of play rather than a world of strife. Each advancement of knowledge symbolizes a freer mind and comprises a greater whole of completion by the enlargement of his conceptual wholes despite the maze of positives and the negatives which challenge and try to frustrate the metaphysical aim of life. At the intellectual stage, the rule of a blind will has partially ended, for here a sentimental man wars as much with ideologies as he does in gladiatorial contests; a newly emerging man of knowledge now vies with both an irrational universe and a blind will for the future of his self or soul as the more mobile patterns seek the larger wholes of experience by means of freedom concepts.

CHAPTER XX

The Pattern of Faith

BESIDES THE MANY other difficulties which confront man in his pursuit of happiness, there always lurks in the foreground the certainty of his earthly doom. When man soberly reflects he realizes that he is but a minor actor in a great drama of creation and destruction; each day that slips away forebodes a tragic end to every man's life. Like all metaphysical movements there is a need for a completion, but for man to symbolize it he must first embody in an ideal or spiritual form that which he considers to be life's full presentation.

As man emerged from out of the darkness of his past he opened the door of intellectual freedom wider by his conception of a spiritual whole of reality. While the belief in another life after death is not held by all cultures of mankind, even in our own day, it nevertheless has its roots deep in antiquity. This has been confirmed by archaeologists who, while digging into the graves of Neanderthals, found evidence that these ancient forerunners of modern man buried the bodies of their dead upright in their graves and supplied them with food for what they presumed was to be a long journey. Unknowingly, perhaps, this early man had made the first attempt to bridge himself over to a spiritual whole of completion. Primitive man was surrounded by mystery; he saw the lightning and heard the thunder and was awed by the majestic parade of ghost-like objects across the day and night skies. It was not long before he sought ways of explaining nature's mysteries, and he later tried to identify himself with them by means of a crude religious belief; eventually some form of religious worship became a part of the life of the tribesman, and many of his customs and laws were built around it.

Man has sought different ways of escaping or explaining the realities of life by various forms of religious belief which have usually led to faith becoming highly organized. Due to the common bond that is forged by religion, such as marriage ceremonies and burial rites, a faith often becomes powerfully organized—"a bulwark of the state that is rigid in its demands and intolerant in its breaches." For lack of something better to lean upon to make life more bearable, man has continued to build his temples and furnish them with gods and devils in an imaginary wonderland that lies beyond the grave; many of the faiths have withstood the ravages of time and their devotees still number in legions, but the faiths most often rest upon the shifting sands of a changing world.

As is true in all processes of life, the pattern of faith as part of the higher releases of life must contend with both the stable and the unstable factors of reality, and it is usually the stable factors that frustrate the will in a more comprehensive completion. When a faith becomes too authoritative, the natural impulsion towards a fuller completion becomes restricted and the movement is slowed as the members of the faith find consolation in a monolithic idealism; thus again, life's urge for completion has found a makeshift haven of stability. The pattern of faith flows freely when permitted to do so. This is true in the development of monotheism, where the early Jehovah was a vengeful God who bestowed his grace only upon the Jewish people; later, however, after their captivity by the Babylonians, their conception of God enlarged and we find Jehovah emerging as a universal God. Later, through Christ, he became a God of Salvation for all Christians.

The love of the beautiful, which slowly developed out of the pattern of form, is incontestable; but faith, which has developed more recently, is also uncontested. For this reason it is difficult to change an organized system of belief sufficiently in order to make it conform to the more flexible conditions of the modern world. There is little room in the modern world for a fixed faith, in which there is a constant enlargement of knowledge which is based upon fact. For this reason faith must keep developing in order to meet the increased demand of a greater intellectual freedom. Despite the reluctance and often timidity of religious leaders to replace the older monolithic idealism with a dynamic and evolving one, progress is being made towards the more enlightened conception of the ideal religion where the older values are replaced with newer ones so long as they lead to a greater whole of completion. The freer and more practical conception is not only influencing and changing the older systems of belief but is revitalizing the entire spiritual movement itself. True religious idealism must enlarge upon the conception of freedom or else relegate man to the dead-end of nature, just as a blind will has for the lower species by destroying the metaphysical basis for faith. Therefore, it is necessary that all faith organizations of the future permit a practical life pattern to direct their metaphysical development through the activation of the finer feelings and to leave the door open for a spiritual whole of harmony. It is interesting to note that such a spiritual being is usually transferable to an idol or human embodiment and the God pattern is symbolized through it.

As a part of the metaphysical aim of life the pattern of faith is necessary to it, and out of it has risen The Image Whole, or a disembodied spirit. Religion as an ideal whole is a projected wish; as a practical whole it is a way of life. Man recognizes life as an unfinished symphony with, perhaps, an impossible finale, but the yearning for the finest completion gives the greatest satisfaction in a world of infinite tension. Man can never attain an ultimate goal of perfection by any faith, but faith as a freedom concept is a part of the stream of religious idealism which furnishes the foundation for the soul to symbolize itself as the forefront of its development. By it, man creates the drama and sets the stage for the most rewarding moments of a comparatively short and incompleted life. Out of the old and too rigid orthodoxy there is being laid the foundation of a new religious idealism that is activated by a practical life-pattern, which gives the individual the freedom to choose his ideal ends without the restrictions of the past so he can continue his search for an ideal completion. Activated sentimentalism as an evolutionary concept of the finer feelings provides the basis for the new faith and gives a unity of purpose to life which we can partially understand as a constructive escape-relief-creation pattern; without it we cannot understand man's religious aspirations at all.

The ideal religion is a pure religion which has been stripped of its dogma and is developing through the enlargement of experience as the pattern of faith keeps pyramiding the life process into a higher balance of harmony. In the inclusive sense, faith is the belief that the final balance of life is attainable and that there will be freedom to reach the goal by means of the finest conceptual values. The will is activated by the higher conceptual values and charges all experience to seek a final solution through the rational as opposed to the irrational. Religious idealism, as a part of the higher releases of life, has developed a soul of harmony with the possibility of infinite good. As the soul idealizes it keeps widening the scope of its activity as it endeavors to achieve the greatest concord of all—the merger of the soul into a spiritual whole by means of unity, symmetry and proportion. Here the spiritually symbolical of the present seeks to become the reality of the future, which reminds us of what the blind will accomplished when it integrated the cosmic pattern of irrationality into the harmoniously functioning organs of the body. But the spiritually symbolical is not a God which is dead, or a stationary God, but a God which is becoming more real as the freedom of man develops.

The future of life has no rational boundary but is an unlimited refining medium for the soul to weave harmonies as it idealizes. Neither is faith stationary and out of tempo with the rest of the universe; it is a rational partner in the quest of a common goal of completion by the processes of infinite patterns. As far as life is concerned it is a continuous process of realization, from the vague and the indistinct to one of full realization and light. The mind of man is a synthesis of freedom concepts which expresses its spirituality through celestial manifestations. A rational man must complete his unity by means of his ideals, for without them there would be no spiritual movement, no soul to ennoble, and he would stand blind and mute before the universe as it irrationally processed itself through its destructive stages and phases of lessening tension. Life by its nature must try to complete itself, although it does not have sufficient experience to complete the picture of an ideal real. Man only knows that he came into being after the universe was created; by necessity, to attain surcease from its tensions, he must project himself against it to eternity if he is to survive.

CHAPTER XXI

The Love of the Beautiful as a Freedom Concept

BASIC TO ALL wholes of completion and belonging to all three metaphysical stages of life is the pattern of form which consists of an infinite variety of unity, symmetry and proportion. It has already been stated that there are as many numbers in the universe as there are escape-relief-creation patterns, and as many systems of thinking possible as there are complex stages; we might further add that there are as many patterns of form possible as there are systems of thinking. We have found a pattern of form displayed at the lowest physical stage of life, where a blind will organizes itself as an instrument of refinement through a built-in process of reasoning: being the foundation of that stage, it is the most recognizable and enduring handiwork of nature. At the instinctive stage it consists of a phase and is not as durable as it is at the physical stage, but we recognize it in the songs of birds. When found at the intellectual stage, the pattern of form is even more fleeting, for here the conscious phase has acquired a soul which must complete itself by means of its idealizations.

Schelling believed that art is the object that nature has in view in all her creations, and he endeavored to fashion all human activity in artistic form. He spoke of the beautiful soul. The aesthetic feelings of the romanticists, however, were capricious and individualistic, and are in sharp contrast to the philosophy of activated sentimentalism. This is an evolutionary concept of the finer feelings which has as its goal a spiritual whole of harmony and is an impulsion for all souls by means of a systematic realism. Well may

Earth have spoken for our voyage in Shelley's *Prometheus Unbound,* when he declares:

> *Man, one harmonious Soul of many a soul,*
> *Whose nature is its own divine control,*
> *Where all things flow to all, as rivers to the sea.*

Ideals as a spiritual embodiment must subsist upon the wholes or contents of the aesthetic feelings which compose their woof and warp through unity, symmetry and proportion. When the psychologist states that the sensuous feelings are steps in the development of the aesthetic feelings, he insists that to be so they must promote ideal ends. This is but another confirmation of our theory that life at its highest and freest manifestation is seeking a hypothetical balance of harmony and must be explained metaphysically as phases and stages of lessening tension that are governed by a practical escape-relief-creation pattern.

Sometimes the naturalist uses the term "sports" or "variants" to imply unusual individual characteristics which may be transmitted and are useful in the development of the species. Due to the greater fluidity of the feeling stream of life, the intellectual stage also has its sports or variants which further the finer feelings and out of which arise the creativity of the artist and the mystic. Often the artist and the mystic relate having feeling breakthroughs that are conducive to a greater creativity. Whether this is due in part to forebears or racial groups that promote the more fluid development of the finer feelings is a theory we shall not be concerned with on the present voyage; but the theory will be advanced that certain feelings rise within the artist or the mystic which cause them to become a sport or variant in which the pattern of form is used for the ideal. Just as a million buds must perish to generate one noble flower, perhaps it takes many wretched Bohemians to produce one noble artist or mystic. While the aptitudes of the artist and the mystic may not be inherited as a biological factor, their imaginative creations become the legacies of all ages.

The terminology of the modern artist includes such

expressions as "reality," "universal," and "abstract," which remind us of many of the terms used on our flght to eternity. The artist, however, is still the child of inspiration and has not yet sensed the possibility and extension of a practical life-pattern which guides all creativity to an ideal conclusion. But the love for the beautiful is not peculiar to the artist and the mystic alone, because we find its growing expression in science and philosophy as well, and such expressions have become a part of the terminology of scientific and philosophical treatises. Since we believe we have established the actual pattern used by both life and the universe and have determined the respective goals of each, we have placed the chapter The Love of the Beautiful as a Freedom Concept near the close of our journey, for "the phase, the stage, the phase" are the essential part of man's metaphysical nature as he idealizes on his way to eternity.

The love for the beautiful is the most universal and primitive of our idealizations. In the contemplation of beauty, the soul finds its most pleasant expression of freedom— a momentary release from the discordance of existence. For it is here that the idealization of man gives vent to the most delightful fancies, which have found expression in poetry, music and painting as well as in many other forms of art. Often the poet expresses the hope and aspirations of all mankind as he relates how the soul of the present-day man is akin to the soul of all ages in its devotion to truth and beauty. In depicting their gods in marble, the Greeks made them more the symbol of beauty and excellence than of worship. "Western art for many centuries found its finest expression in the music, painting, sculpture and architecture of the Church; the love for the beautiful came to mean the same as the love for God—an expression of the absolute when there was little else to convey the meaning to the poorly learned members, a part of the haven that the early Christians longed to reach."—Dewey.

Because the practical and the ideal tend to draw closer in the movement of life, the closing of the gap becomes manifest in the final stages of a civilization. As wealth increases and man is able to escape from monotony and a world of toil, he seeks further expression of freedom in things of beauty. The use of art in commercial advertising attests to its widespread appeal in modern-day living, and there is a demand for a greater freedom in its expression. The politician's sponsorship of the "city beautiful" and urban renewal programs demonstrates the popularity of these ideas among the voting masses. Perhaps one of Western civilization's greatest contributions to art is that it has spread the love for the beautiful to more classes of people than any other civilization of the past.

CHAPTER XXII

General Summary and Conclusion

THE VOYAGE must end now. We have reached eternity, the last tension area of the universe, and we dare not go further; for here all things end, including the processes of knowledge. During the voyage we have followed the course of the irrational universe as it tries to stabilize itself through ephemeral wholes of a destructive reality; we have seen how a blind will rationally seeks surcease from the irrationalism of the universe by positing its patterns of harmony against it; and we have theorized that as it did so it developed into higher metaphysical stages of development. On the last lap of our journey we have witnessed the rise of a partially free man and how he endeavors to complete himself by means of his idealizations—the very need for the consummation of the life process provides the impulsion for the movement.

During our flight we have tried to show that neither the destructive movement of the universe nor the constructive movement of life can be explained solely in terms of physical reality. If they are to be explained they must be explained as stages and phases or phases and stages of lessening tension that is governed by the primal escape-relief-creation pattern. It has further been contended that the movement of both life and the universe is seeking a hypothetical or ultimate completion, and as they systematically release themselves from tension they flow more freely as processed realities. In order to construct a metaphysical framework for the universe it has been deemed best to separate the processed reality from a nonprocessed unreality and to imagine the latter as a uniphase which consists of a patternless stream of motion that is purely creative by obeying the Law of Resistance to Change of Motion, the law that ties the unreal to the real. As the unreality, it consists of a variable negation of an inverted stream of motion that was jammed into a plus and minus balance—the unit of the cosmic—which was later distorted into the escape-relief-creation pattern of the universal reality. The unit was never a part of the universe as the unsplintered balance but became a part of it by being splintered into the neutrinos and photons of the giant universal atom which formed the elements for the expanding universe.

After the pattern was formed out of the disruption of the unit it took over the task of governing all the reality-wholes of the universe by slowly reducing their energy as it overcame the universal Law of Resistance to Change of Motion throughout a complexity of stages and phases; however, the movement remains largely unresolved and continues to seek the more stable conditions of an ultimate negation. The universe that was created became a processed one of fleeting reals, always on the move and continually seeking a balance of its stable and unstable factors—a multiplicity of tension centers that are infinitely large and infinitely small. The pattern became the universal Law of Consistency and the stable and unstable factors behind each reality-whole necessitated the continuance in The Flight From Tension. The pattern that governs the release of all energy is not a rigid one, and as the tensions of the reality movement lessen, the escape phase is less frequent, the relief is longer and the creation is more widespread. However, the movement is completed as far as possible in each whole and the residue goes to form another triad that continues to seek further completion and which creates the evolutionary movement to eternity, the end of the tension line. The complexity of the universe is due to the diversity and the intensity of its pressures and not to the consistent pattern that governs the movement to completion. Such factors as cause-space-time belong exclusively to the universe and vanish at the last line of tension, where all reality ends.

After a period the earth's surface cooled, and with other

favorable conditions a part of the destructive process was reversed and played against itself. It was then that an inverted pattern became the will of life. The reality of life consists of phases and stages of lessening tensions or harmonies that were forcibly organized as a necessity of refinement, and it comprises the category of refinement which is a built-in process of reasoning at every metaphysical stage of life. Because of the need for the completion of the life-process, the universe acquired a counter-partner, for the will was forced to match its phases and stages against the stages and phases of cosmic urgency. The parent is irrational with its child, for the will must always posit its rationality against the parent's irrationality, and as it does so it creates the world of experience and knowledge. In the course of the evolution of life the will has pyramided the process through more than two billion years of intense struggle consisting of violent geographical and climatic changes. Out of the rational movement there developed many species with their endless adaptations, and as an imperative for refinement life has developed from a one-cell organism to the dominant intellectual man of today.

In the course of its long evolution life increased its mobility in three metaphysical stages of development—the physical, the instinctive and the intellectual, which are the fundamental balances of life. The physical is basic to all stages in order to prevent their sudden completion. But as the metaphysical stream of life became increasingly accelerated, animal organisms were able to promote and sustain a blind phase that is emotional in nature and is stabilized or balanced by the instinctive stage. However, when its routine is disturbed it must surge to a higher intellectual stage for correction. Both the physical and the instinctive stages are blindly rational, but the intellectual stage is partially free due to a sustained phase of conscious reasoning.

The intellectual stage consists of a process of conscious reasoning with plans to relieve the tensions of life. Ideas with plans to relieve tension require a wide latitude for their activity in order to achieve the finer balances which the will persists in creating. With their many plans to relieve the tensions of life, ideas create the concept of good and bad, true and false, to the extent of their success or failure in accomplishing their task.

The conscious process is a metaphysical stream which is seeking completion and consists of the constant adjustment between the objective states of existence and the subjective phase of being. At the intellectual stage the process of reasoning can take the discordant emotions and distinguish or differentiate them into a variety of feelings. The self or soul, being the embodiment of the conscious stream, is continually being activated towards a hypothetical balance of harmony by the development of the finer feelings; which, if possible of attainment, would consist of an ideal or spiritual realm.

Metaphysically, life is a release from blindness through evolutionary development towards a hypothetical balance of harmony by a practical escape-relief-creation pattern which is manifested throughout life; by the urgency for refinement and the increasingly freer releases, each metaphysical stage represents a greater whole of completion. While no form or ideal is ever completely realized it must always have that possibility; the graveyard of biological failures is filled with species that did not have the flexibility to meet a new challenge with a larger whole of reality.

The will has taken all the discordance of existence and pieced it into a mosaic which reflects the faith and hopes of its continuance. Life, with its values which have been inherited from the travail of the past, is not a sham reality; through the creation of fresher patterns it has been able to hand to the next generation a new value which can still be developed into something higher. The higher life has developed, the more sublime has become its spiritual goal, until the image-whole is no longer stationary and out of step with the metaphysical aim of life but is an integral part of it. Today, the older rigid faiths are being replaced by a dynamic and evolving one and, as a result of this, man is becoming more rational, with a clearer conception of the goal of life and its relationship to that of the universe. Mankind is moving into a new era of enlightenment, but it must take the fullest advantage of all human resources and eliminate the time and effort wasted on superstition and false ideologies. Like the primitive man, modern man is still a new frontiersman, seeking not just new lands to settle but new ideas that will afford a greater stability to society and will become a part of tomorrow's higher plateau. But the older plateau must first be cleared of false ideologies. If man is to continue his development as a rational being, he must retain his freedom of action at all costs; the torch of intellectual freedom is in his hands, and should he relinquish his right to freedom, he will go the way of all dead-ends of nature and become merely a negative of the cosmic way.

Man is sustained by his faith, his courage and his love; take them away and he will become an empty shell without further incentive for striving. Should he ever embrace a creed whereby he thinks that he is but a pawn of fate and is hopelessly entangled in an enigma which is itself wrapped in a mystery and out of which he can never hope to extricate himself, then life will no longer be worthwhile; pessimism will have won its battle over optimism, for discordance will overtake the harmony that life is seeking, and feeling, which gives conscious value to life, will become meaningless. Then, a partially free man with his strong urge for completion will have fallen victim to his own rationality, leaving the world again to the irrationalism of the universe and the rationalization of a blind will that would be satisfied with the minimum harmony of existence. Throughout the long history of life and up to the present, at least, optimism has had the better of the argument. It has always been able to create something new, which is a little better, finer and more complete and which gives form to life through unity, symmetry and proportion and furnishes a springboard for the whole movement as man continues to pursue his search for a hypothetical balance.